MAJOR PROBLEMS
IN CONTEMPORARY
EUROPEAN PHILOSOPHY

Ludwig Landgrebe

MAJOR PROBLEMS IN CONTEMPORARY EUROPEAN PHILOSOPHY

From Dilthey to Heidegger

Translated from the German by
KURT F. REINHARDT

FREDERICK UNGAR PUBLISHING CO.
NEW YORK

Printed in the United States of America

Library of Congress Catalog Card No. 64-25558

PREFACE

Ludwig Landgrebe, born in 1902, is Professor of Philosophy at the University of Cologne. He is known in Europe as one of the main representatives of *Phenomenology,* that school of philosophy which was founded by Edmund Husserl (1859-1938) who, together with Henri Bergson, is credited with having brought about that "resurrection of metaphysics" which marks a radical break with positivistic "scientism" in European thought. The pioneer work done by Husserl and his associates and followers in leading Western philosophy back to the sources of all "essential" or "foundational" thinking is bearing fruit in increasing measure not only on the European Continent but also in England and in the Americas. The "phenomenological method" has been appropriated by the proponents of "existentialism" or the Philosophy of Existence in both its atheistic and theistic-Christian branches, and the impact of "existential phenomenology" is felt most strongly in psychiatry and psychotherapy.

Ludwig Landgrebe was Husserl's research assistant from 1923 to 1930 and is internationally known for his association with the Husserl Archives of Cologne and Louvain and as the editor of some of Husserl's posthumously published works. Among Landgrebe's own independent publications the collection of essays entitled *Phänomenologie und Metaphysik* (1949) and the work presented here in English translation—originally published under the title *Philosophie der Gegenwart* (1957)—are of special significance in their exploration of entirely new dimensions in contemporary European philosophy. The latter work in particular is primarily not a "survey" of a multiplicity of intellectual movements and schools of thought, but rather a highly successful attempt at analyzing the problems that are the motivating forces animating and agitating the contemporary philosophic spectrum in all its breadth and depth—problems of vital concern to everyone because they present a bold challenge to every kind of hardened traditionalism.

Interwoven with the author's lucid presentation of the new departures in the several fields of the natural and humanistic sciences is an equally clear-sighted and convincingly substantiated critical appraisal of the most important thinkers of the twentieth century, from Dilthey, Driesch, Heisenberg, Schrödinger to Scheler, Nicolai Hartmann, Sartre, Camus, Marcel, Husserl and Heidegger—to name only the most prominent in their respective fields. The main themes of Landgrebe's cross-section of contemporary European thought are centered in chapters that deal specifically with the nature of man, the concept of "world," the "world" of natural science, the philosophic problems of art and literature, the interrelation of thought and action, and the "problem of Being" in its relation to philosophy and theology.

The translator gratefully acknowledges his indebtedness to Mrs. Florence Brokmeyer for substantial aid in preparing the manuscript for the publisher; and to Miss Joyce Eileen McKee, Miss Judy Dunbar, and Mr. John Hibbard for their assistance in revising the notes and the bibliography and preparing the index.

KURT F. REINHARDT

Stanford University, California
January 4, 1966

CONTENTS

INTRODUCTION

An introduction to Contemporary Philosophy has to contend with a number of difficulties. They are caused, first, by the nature of philosophic thinking in general, since everyone seems to take it for granted that he is to a greater or lesser extent familiar with it, although this supposed familiarity may turn out to be no more than a series of preconceived opinions. Secondly, these difficulties result from the peculiar situation in which philosophy finds itself today. This situation is characterized by a radical reexamination of the very foundations of philosophic thinking, foundations which have accumulated in the course of a historical tradition which spans two and a half millennia. For even in Kant's lifetime the ancient "scholastic" division of philosophy into individual disciplines—which made it possible to assign to each problem its proper place—had become fluid. Again and again new disciplines have been added (e.g., epistemology or the "theory of knowledge," or "philosophic anthropology"), each of them claiming to be capable of stepping into the position formerly held by metaphysics as the basic philosophical discipline. And this despite the fact that any agreement concerning the interrelationship of these disciplines, their mutual boundaries, or even concerning the meaning of such a division of philosophy into separate disciplines was lacking. Precisely where philosophy in its queries penetrates farthest it becomes evident that this division tends to fracture the frame of each individual discipline and that there exist in philosophy no "special" or "separate" problems which could be discussed and comprehended without being referred to its whole and individual essence.

This is the reason why an introduction to Contemporary Philosophy cannot take as its guide some arbitrary division according to individual disciplines, with the intent of simply asking how much "progress" has been made in these disciplines during the past decades. Nor can such an introduction confine itself to presenting with the greatest possible "neutrality" the actual "schools" of vital philosophic thought and a classification according to different "trends" or "movements." Although, as far as the author of such an introduction is concerned, this may appear as the most convenient and least perilous procedure, the one least apt to arouse negative criticism (provided that the enumeration is complete, that nothing has been forgotten or omitted and that every thinker has received his due), it would certainly put the reader into the embarrassing position of having been served with a non-committal survey of a great many "movements," "schools," and "isms," without any guideposts that would permit him to orient himself in this confusing jungle. Such a procedure would only strengthen the mistaken opinion that philosophy is essentially a struggle of different views of life *(Weltanschauungen)* and systems of thought, among whom everyone may freely choose the one that suits him best. It is precisely this kind of willful arbitrariness *(Unverbindlichkeit)* which has brought philosophy into the odious repute of being nothing but a useless intellectual game. This situation makes mandatory a basic reappraisal of the nature of philosophy and of its traditional foundations. This attempt in turn has had the result that philosophy, instead of dealing with specific problems, has become preoccupied with reflections on its own nature, with attempts at justifying itself and its tasks and function in society. In doing this, philosophy has shown itself to be the true expression of an age which no longer succeeds in presenting to itself—by means of reflection—an unclouded mirror of its being. The dimming and eventual shattering of this mirror corresponds to the fractured state of philosophy itself which in its attempted self-understanding has become questionable to itself, finding itself no longer capable of establishing some firm ground upon which it might gain certitude as to where it stands and whither it intends to go.

What is needed to do justice to this situation is a presentation which is not oriented according to "disciplines" and "schools" or "movements" but is interested in those *vital problems* which are the prime movers of current philosophic thought—problems which are not merely discussed because philosophy in tis very existence represents a venerable tradition that *ipso facto* includes these problems, but because they are *our* problems and because their resolution concerns *all of us*. It is this point of view which of necessity serves us as a principle of selection and organization.

This introduction will then attempt to present the evolution of contemporary philosophy as a trail which *leads to one fundamental problem* that is inseparably related to the total situation of our time. It will try to understand the tendencies of present day philosophy as a unified movement, as the beginning of a decisive change, the necessity of which is already universally felt and the meaning of which manifests itself clearly and visibly in philosophic thought. In accepting this *de facto* change as something that cannot be disputed, this introduction, to be sure, intends to be more than a "neutral" presentation: it advances a very definite *position*. Taking such a "position," however, is something different from adopting a "point of view": taking a "position" is of the very essence of philosophy and is necessitated by the fact that philosophic problems cannot be posited arbitrarily and "without any presuppositions" *(voraussetzungslos)* but are genuinely philosophical only in those instances where they have as their object matters which have become problematic for human existence within the frame of reference of the particular stress and distress of a historical situation. The term "present age" *(Gegenwart)* should therefore not be understood in an external chronological sense but as designating the unity of a specific historical situation. And only with a view to such a historical situation can it be determined what must be included in the frame of "contemporary philosophy." If it should be asked what in this case becomes of the so-called "eternal" questions of philosophy, we reply that this "eternity" is not a kind of possession that is available at any time but rather implies the unbroken continuity of a task whose urgency can disclose or reveal itself in ever novel ways only within a given historical situation.

Such a procedure will of course always provoke the reproach of arbitrariness and onesidedness, for it presupposes as a matter of course a definite *intrepretation* regarding the meaning of the historical evolution of philosophy. We may legitimately ask whether it is, after all, certain that ideas which make their appearance with the pretense of a radical subversion of the philosophic tradition, cannot themselves be proven to be mere variations of those familiar *schemata* and antitheses which since time immemorial have determined philosophic thought. It would seem, however, that it is more fruitful to subject new ideas to philosophic reflection and meditation than to attempt a classification in accord with some traditional *schemata*. If we proceed in this manner, we will best prepare ourselves for the truth of the fact that in philosophy, too, the saying that "everything has happened before" is invalid. This introduction, therefore, expects to be evaluated as nothing more than a tentative preliminary step forward, for it would indeed be presumptuous—in consideration of the situation of contemporary philosophy—to make definitive pronouncements concerning the meaning of the general trend of present day philosophy. If we were to succeed in this presentation to prepare the ground for an adequate factual discussion, we would feel that the maximal aim of this endeavor has been fulfilled.

From the intrinsic essential relationship that exists between philosophic problems and the particular historical situations of the questioning philosopher it follows that in our presentation the developments within the frame of *German* philosophy must occupy a central position and that the situation of philosophy in other countries can be considered only to the extent that it is vitally and reciprocally related to German thought. We must therefore plead guilty if the reader accuses us of having omitted a discussion of some significant and exemplary thinkers in non-German regions. For if we want to avoid a mere superficially cataloguing survey and orientation, our presentation must start out from what is nearest to us, that is, from *our own tradition* and the situation produced by it. That which is farther removed can be appropriated only to the extent that our own perspectives permit access to it. In this way only will we be able to see a reciprocal give-and-take and will we begin to appreciate the common and mutually shared destiny of the West. This common destiny is grounded in a common origin and tradition and though these common features have become—especially since the end of the eighteenth century—more and more blurred and almost obliterated, they stand out all the more clearly today, at a time when the West is faced with the greatest crisis in its history. This crisis, which will decide about the status and stature of man in the near and even distant future, was bound to grow to universal proportions in the measure in which the rest of our world was seized by the preponderant power of technology. And if it be true that the dictatorial claims of technology can be understood only by viewing it as originating from basic ideas embodied in Western Philosophy and in specific epistemological tenets founded upon them—an assertion which, to be sure, can be substantiated only in the context of our presentation (cf. Chap. VI)—then the resulting crisis can be overcome only by a radically penetrating inquiry into these origins. The critical reflection on the hidden ultimate presuppositions of Western thought which has had its beginnings in contemporary German philosophy, may therefore—if it actually leads to the dimly envisaged goal—mean much more than a mere re-formation of philosophy.

So far we have been sketching *the situation* which must be faced by philosophic thought if it wants to advance an authentic claim to true actuality *(Gegenwärtigkeit),* and we have to name *the principle* which is to guide our selective procedure. It is unavoidable that the reasons for proceeding in this particular manner derive their support from an assertion of certain constellations which can be verified only by a perusal of this book in its entirety, notwithstanding the fact that this may lead to the suspicion that "the subject matter itself, even in the totality of its essence, is compressed and fully expressed in the intentional goal or in the final results" [1] of this investigation. We therefore advise the reader not to take these introductory remarks for more than they intend to be: indispensable preliminary pointers, indicative of the general plan of this treatise.

If we want, first of all, to describe the common ground on which European philosophy and the thinkers determined by it rests, we may say that it is characterized throughout by the elimination of an attitude which had gained its maximum momentum at the end of the nineteenth century, an attitude which can be designated as *positivistic* in the most comprehensive sense of the term. Gaston Berger, for example, states in his survey of contemporary French philosophy [2] that none of the currently representative French thinkers can be said to accept the doctrines of a naive positivism which recognizes  as meaningful and intelligible only that which can ultimately be reduced and tested by sensory experience. This kind of positivism regards it as self-evident that all truly existing entities are material in their nature, either in accord with the teachings of a crude materialism or a sensism which regards only the data of sensation as the truly "real." In this latter case the concept of the sensed data is determined by its correlative relationship to objectively and physically comprehensible sense stimuli issuing from matter. *Logical Positivism*—which asserts the purely operational or instrumental nature of the functions of knowledge—represents a necessary complement of this kind of either materialist or sensist positivism. It regards logical thinking as an all-powerful instrument whose functioning is entirely determined by convention and by means of which the amorphous reality is to be grasped and ordered by the firm grip of thought. Logical Positivism may thus be tied either to a spiritualism which conceives of that which really and truly *is* as resulting from the ordering and regulating power of the logico-mathematically operating mind, or to a pragmatism and refined materialism which see in thought nothing but an instrument of self-affirmation on the part of a specific genus of living being and regard the formation of any concepts which transcend the orientational functions of thinking as meaningless. This makes it possible to understand the peculiar affinity that exists between Logical Positivism and the doctrines of Marxism. In Chapter VI we shall demonstrate how in these trends of thought a development that can be traced back to the beginning of modern times has come to its fruition. The common denominator is the absolutization of the logico-mathematical method and its application to the realm of the natural sciences as well as the unquestioning acceptance of the "exact sciences" as the absolute model of all science, including philosophy.

If, in opposition to this point of view, we want to describe *a common basic characteristic of present day European philosophy,* we may state that the turning away from positivism signifies at the same time the total abandonment of the opinion that the scientific nature of philosophy could be gauged by using the "objective" and especially the "exact" sciences as a standard of measurement. It should be observed, however, that North-American philosophy has on the whole not followed the path of these European developments. Although it is correct to say that in the many-sided physiognomy of American intellectual life almost all the shades of European trends of thought are represented, Pragmatism and Logical Positivism are nonetheless the two prevalent basic tendencies which seem to correspond most closely to a deeply rooted particular characteristic of the American mentality and of the manner in which Americans understand themselves. British philosophy, too, proceeds by and large on its own road, in separation from the continental-European developments, and as a consequence there are few mutual relations between British and German contemporary philosophy, aside from the research in the fields of logic and the history of philosophy. South American philosophy, on the other hand, is almost completely determined by the problems posed in present day European thinking, as was amply demonstrated on the occasion of the first South American Congress of Philosophy (held in Argentina in 1949).

It is furthermore characteristic of present-day European philosophy that historic materialism, too, has failed to arrive at any developments or solutions which could be termed essentially new. Even in its most important representations it has shown itself incapable of progressing beyond the foundations laid by Karl Marx. In its materialistic outlook it has become more and more rigidly dogmatic and shallow and has thus not succeeded in following the original intuitions of Marx who in his youth had understood his philosophic endeavors as a kind of "realistic humanism," as an inquiry into the nature of concrete human existence. Where, on the other hand, Marxism was able to free itself from such rigid dogmatism, it succeeded in giving new impulses to the Sociology of Knowledge.

In *German* philosophy this movement away from positivism and materialism and from the guiding ideal of the exact sciences that took place in the period following World War I, was interpreted as a "resurrection of metaphysics" (this was the title of a frequently quoted book by Peter Wust). This turning away finds its explanation in a change of position on several points. The shaken complacency of the blind scientific optimism that characterized the period preceding World War I called in question the definition of the nature of philosophy as a mere scientific theory and a mere epistemological critique *(Wissenschaftstheorie und Erkenntniskritik),* which was current and unquestioned at the turn of the century. This shaking of a naive confidence aroused a consciousness of the insufficiency of mere methodological discussions and disputations concerning the problem of the possibility of valid scientific and philosophic knowledge—a characteristic feature especially of Neo-Kantianism. The "hunger for reality," for "unabridged reality," which began to assert itself more and more vigorously, led to the demand for a direct encounter with "the things themselves" *(mit den "Sachen selbst")*—a watchword which had already been proclaimed by the positivism of the late nineteenth century (and which the positivists had interpreted in their *own* way) but which subsequently was appropriated by Edmund Husserl and incorporated in his Phenomenology.[3]

This demand meant that the world and existing entities in their totality must no longer be accepted in the interpretation they had undergone at the hands of science and philosophy (as if it could be taken for granted that the "scientific world view" encompassed the world as such), but the questioning must penetrate beyond and behind this interpretation: it must be asked what these entities are prior to their scientific and philosophic interpretation, while the interpretation itself must be understood as resulting from the encounter of "life" and "world." Whereas for the late nineteenth century the world as interpreted by science and philosophy and the culture that reflected it had been the ultimate unquestioned facticity, the movement initiated after the end of World War I may be regarded as the result of the definitive breakdown of this kind of interpretation. The "resurrection of metaphysics" can therefore be understood in a dual sense: first, as a "turning toward the object," toward entities in all their manifoldness and essential determinants, so that the main theme of this resurrection appeared to be the essence of things (set and thought apart from their "existence"" which can be grasped in an "essential intuition" (*Wesensanschauung*) [4]; second, as *a return to the living subject* and its formative activity, considered as the "ground" or ultimate *raison d'être* of all the forms of culture, philosophy, and science.

The *direction of this return* is determined and limited by the horizons which had been pre-formed by the intellectual and cultural climate of the nineteenth century. Whereas in the Philosophy of Hegel the subject had been defined as the Absolute Spirit—a definition which once again (and, as far as the nineteenth century is concerned, for the last time) offered an answer to the ancient quest of metaphysics for the Supreme Existent Entity, the remainder of the nineteenth century evolved in the shadow of the decisive event of the breakdown of German idealism. It was this same idealism which had delineated for the man of the nineteenth century the horizons that became binding for his self-interpretation and therewith had prepared the way for that new situation which made a "resurrection of metaphysics" possible. This new situation was determined, on the one hand, by the continuing effects of the criticism which the Young Hegelians launched against Hegel. This critique generated the conviction—accepted almost as self-evident—that the Supreme Existing Entity sought by metaphysics—the principle which could explain the essence and origin of all existing entities—could not possibly be a thing-in-itself, a substance, or an Absolute Spirit. That which was termed "absolute spirit" must rather be nothing but a hypostasis of the human mind which was bound to recognize itself as the ultimate principle of any explication. Thus, beginning with Ludwig Feuerbach, *man* moves into the center of philosophy, and *anthropology* steps into the place of metaphysics as the basic philosophic discipline.[5]

The new thesis was programmatically stated by Karl Marx when he said: "We must peel out of the divinized forms their earthy kernel," that is, we must learn to understand man as a being who produces himself and his world. On this foundation rest all the attempts to reduce the forms of religion, of the state, of civilization and culture in general to the formative activity of man. Simultaneously, however, the concept of man itself is being relativized: the essence of man is understood as subject to a historically conditioned unfolding and change, and from this results finally the conviction of the *relativity* of all the forms of civilization within the frame of reference of the historically evolving human nature and essence. This conviction is generally known as "historicism" (*Historismus*).

Anthropology and *historicism* are thus the points of view which determine the horizon within which the return of philosophy to metaphysics took place after the end of World War I. They directed the resumption of the metaphysical quest for some ultimate principle and for the forward movement of the philosophic questioning beyond the limitations imposed by a purely scientific interpretation of the world. In other words, the "turning toward the object" and the rediscovery of metaphysics bore the earmarks of that decisive encounter with historicism which in the period following World War I was considered of momentous importance. But after historicism had submerged the essence of man himself in the current of history and had relativized the absolute validity of the traditional definition of man as *animal rationale,* the meaning of the metaphysical quest for some ultimate principle was understood as a forward thrust into the realm of the irrational. The real theme of metaphysics, however, and even its very concept remained insufficiently defined, as a consequence of this re-actively gained interpretation. Although the forward thrust into the irrational was impelled by the desire to transcend the narrow boundaries of a questioning limited by anthropology and historicism, it remained of necessity attached to that which it wanted to overcome. How are we to understand this statement, and where do we find evidence for such an attachment?

In the course of the inquiry into the nature of man, prompted and guided by anthropology and historicism, it had already become evident that *every predication concerning man*—even a "purely" objective-scientific predication in the positivistic sense—*implied some basic metaphysical position.* Of this fact, to be sure, positivism was and remained unaware; it rather believed to be rid of *all* metaphysical presuppositions. The turning back to metaphysics, therefore, could not simply amount to a restoration of one of those metaphysical systems whose conflicting and changing claims had characterized the history of modern thought and whose limitations and one-sidedness had become manifest in their historical foundering. But modern thought—as a reactive movement—had nonetheless been unable to free itself from its attachment to this tradition of metaphysical speculation: it left unfinished the presuppositions implicit in this tradition, simply because these presuppositions appeared to be self-evident to such a degree that they did not even rise to the level of consciousness. They were presuppositions and premises which derived from the manner in which Descartes's turning back to the *ego cogito* laid the ground for modern philosophy and its fluctuating metaphysical systems. Descartes, says Hegel, "was one of those human beings who make a totally fresh start." However, this new beginning as such injected its weight and prejudice into the definition of the nature of man and his relationship to all entities, so that subsequently man in the core of his personality was understood as a *subject* which stood over against a world understood as the totality of *objects*. This impressed upon modern philosophy the stamp of "subjectivity." [6]

Thus the "resurrection of metaphysics" could interpret the meaning of its inquiry in the nature of worldly entities only as a "turning toward the object" which occurred within the frame of the subject-object dichotomy; and after the foundering of the ancient concept of metaphysics, understood as a rational discipline—a concept which had been nurtured and grown within this frame—the aim and end of the metaphysical query could be relegated to the realm of the irrational. Herewith, however, the seed whose growth was to break this narrow frame, had already been planted in the incipient return to metaphysics. For this return could not possibly reach its goal as long as even the most hidden presuppositions—that is, the suppositions which had caused the foundering of the metaphysics of the past and its fluctuating systems—were not recognized and annulled. The preconceived judgments or prejudices of which we have spoken were, after all, no mere harmless questions of terminology: they rather had forced the philosophic view into a certain direction in which neither the concept of man nor the concept of the world could be adequately determined.

What, then, remains when none of these historical determinations can any longer be taken as a guide, when all of them have to be called in question? Nothing remains save the problematic or questionable nature of human existence *(Dasein)*—an existence which in none of these determinations can find a guide for a human self-understanding that does justice to the human situation. And thus man—with all the questions he asks of himself and of the world—finds himself *thrown back upon the naked "that-ness," the naked "facticity" of his existence as the ultimate starting point of every philosophic reflection.* And the process whereby man becomes conscious of this situation is the basic trait of contemporary thought: from this absolute zero point it attempts to attain to a new and original beginning. When we hear it occasionally said that only now the problem of man has acquired sufficient maturity,[7] this means that only now the real significance of the trend toward anthropology—which determined man's destiny since the breakdown of idealism—and its defeat by the return to metaphysics becomes visible. This is taking place in a movement of thought which, more radically than former endeavors, envisages the totality of the tradition of Western thought and attempts to make visible its hidden and stifling presuppositions. It thereby tries to understand the real reason for the foundering of the systems of the past, and it thus realizes and judges the result of a development, the meaning of which anthropology and its counterpart (the return to metaphysics) were unable to understand in its full significance. As a consequence, it is not possible for contemporary thought to go straightforward to the "things themselves," as if these "things" were clearly and openly manifest or could be brought into unveiled view by simple methodological devices. It is much more correct to say that contemporary thought can gain its proper posture only in a continuing and continuous dialectic encounter with the total tradition of metaphysical speculation. Only in this way can the concept of metaphysics obtain that precision which it needs if the philosophic inquiry is not to begin haphazardly and is not to proceed along the obscure path of hidden presuppositions. If this goal is to be reached, the significance of the fact that philosophy almost from time immemorial had its center in metaphysics and that the core of metaphysics was the inquiry into the nature of "being" must be understood. This *inquiry into the nature of being* is thus of central significance in the history of metaphysical thinking. And a clarification of the meaning of this inquiry can only take place in the encounter with the tradition of Western thought; it will then depend entirely on the radicalism with which the inquiry is being conducted to what extent philosophy will be capable of gaining a new and firm ground.

The necessity to proceed in this manner explains also why in our own inquiry we cannot simply talk about contemporary thought without making intelligible the situation in which it finds itself at each and every juncture of its historical evolution. Only thus will it become possible to recognize the situation of philosophic thought that is characteristic of the present age. This situation shows clearly that it is no longer possible to maintain the traditional separation between systems of thought and the history of philosophy, since every historical investigation must be at heart intentionally systematic, while conversely every systematic investigation is bound to receive its initial impetus from an encounter with history. There is no doubt, on the other hand, that the purely philological-historical labor of making accessible and of actually sifting the historically transmitted texts, the exploration of their historical origins and of the major influences that have been at work, will always remain the indispensable task of an auxiliary philosophic discipline—a task which in Germany has not received due attention during the past few decades. However, a discussion of the present status of philosophico-historical research falls outside the frame of our current investigation.

What, then, is the real objective of this treatise? We shall attempt to describe the process of the dissolution of the traditional schemata of thought and the forward thrust toward a new kind of inquiry into the nature of being that issues from the ultimate *datum* of human existence, based on those fundamental problems in whose development the meaning of this movement is most clearly in evidence. The references to thinkers and their works must in this context of necessity remain incomplete and can, on account of the brevity of this treatise, have only an exemplary kind of significance. In line with what we have stated before, it is hardly necessary to emphasize again that the problems under discussion cannot be classified as "special problems" and as such be harnessed to the schema of traditional philosophic disciplines. They are in their sum total only *variations, as it were, of the one basic theme of philosophy*. And, if the homogeneous development of thought is to become visible, all of them must be referred back to that one basic theme, namely, the inquiry into the nature of "being" *(Sein)*. In endeavoring to do this, occasional repetitions cannot be avoided.

The necessary continuous references to the historical origins of the problems under discussion compel us to presuppose on the part of the reader an at least elementary familiarity with the history of philosophy. Regrettable as this may seem, it is nonetheless unavoidable; for an attempt on our part to supply this kind of knowledge in the course of our discussion would of course carry us far beyond the limited frame of this brief and summary account.

In some quarters the fact that a presentation of the crucial problems in the field of logic is missing may be regarded as a shortcoming. However, research in this field is on the whole preoccupied with the continuation and further elaboration of the problems of logical syntax and of mathematical logic. Such a discussion presupposes an audience of connoisseurs and could not be dealt with adequately within our limited space. We therefore refer the interested reader to the specialized literature in this particular field. The number of works, on the other hand, which deal extensively with the principles of the problems of logic in general is very small, and the few works which are available have until now exerted very little influence on the progress of research in the field of logic.

It was absolutely necessary, on the other hand, to comment in all brevity on the philosophic significance of present-day developments in the natural sciences. Being a layman in the fields of the natural sciences, the author is of course conscious of the risk he incurs in offering such a comment. However, even where his remarks meet with opposition and criticism, they may at least serve as suggestions and contributions to the currently unavoidable endeavor to aid in the restoration of vital links between the historically conditioned problems of philosophic thought and the evolution and progress in scientific methodology.

CHAPTER I

The Nature *(das Wesen)* of Man

The question as to the nature of man is not merely *one* among many other philosophical questions. If we place it at the head of our discussion of the problems of contemporary philosophy, this should not be taken as an affirmation of that particular trend of the nineteenth century which raised anthropology to the status of the basic philosophic discipline. The pre-eminence of this question is not conditioned by a specific historical period but should rather be understood as pointing to the fundamental fact that in each and every philosophic question man himself is either implicitly or explicitly called in question. For philosophic reflection takes its start at a point where the unquestioned matter-of-course givenness of some world-order in which man feels himself inserted, has been shaken. Once this has occurred, man in his reflective thought seeks to re-ascertain this world-order, so that cognitively he may regain the security of his existence. Even though in this thinking process man does not immediately and explicitly become the theme of a philosophic query—the query being at first rather concerned with the origin of all that which is, including man himself, and with the interpretation of this origin mediated by a Supreme Being—he is nonetheless in his striving for a secure hold the initially hidden motivating force of all this questioning. From the manner in which these questions are being asked and answered, man's relationship to reality can be gauged.

A discussion of the question concerning the nature of man in contemporary philosophy can thus not merely refer to the *doctrines* which are being advanced. These doctrines must rather be examined with a view to the *basic situation of present day man* in relation to total reality as well as in relation to himself, relationships which are mirrored in these doctrines. It will be the objective of this first chapter to demonstrate that this basic situation is undergoing a transformation which is a preliminary step toward that radical revolution which characterizes the self-interpretation of modern man. The following chapters will try to illustrate to what extent this transformation permeates and dominates also all the other problems and fields of present-day thinking.

The prevalent tendency of modern thought—the tendency whose reversal has engendered the crisis of contemporary philosophy—is determined by the speculation of Descartes. Cartesian philosophy has given a definite direction to the question concerning the nature of man, a direction which was adhered to until Hegel's death. Descartes's recourse to the self-assured certitude of the *ego cogito* as the ultimate and indubitable foundation of all knowledge, signifies far more than merely the inauguration of a method of critical epistemological reflection. It is indicative of the decisive event when man, after the breakdown of a world-order determined by Divine Providence, was seeking a new anchor for his existence. However, what happened here—at the beginning of modern times—as a consequence of the disintegration of the medieval world view is quite different from that solitary forlornness which invades human existence following the total dissolution of an ancient, firmly established world order that rested upon religious faith and tradition. In the age of Descartes this event did not result in skepticism and resignation but rather in the unleashing of new and unheard of energies, so that for a long time to come this emancipation of man from the shackles of the Middle Ages was seen exclusively in its positive aspects, that is, not only as a liberation *from* the obligatory character of the claimed absoluteness of the truth of Christian revelation but simultaneously as a liberation of man *for* the no less absolute certitude of the conviction of being able to become his own lawgiver by virtue of his reasoning faculty.[8]

It was this *idea of the autonomy of man* which—after the disintegration of the medieval world—made it possible for him to gain a new hold, a new security of his existence. This possibility became an actuality owing to the fact that an idea—which itself originated in the soil of the outgrown tradition—was firmly adhered to, the idea namely that man, on account of his being created in the image and likeness of God, must above all be regarded and esteemed as a rational being. He could therefore found his existence upon the self-assured certitude of reason and its clear and distinct cognition. If it is thus this idea which determines the basic relationship of modern man to reality, then the transformation which he is undergoing in our time can be understood as the *"crisis of reason."* [9] It is a crisis which came to a head not subsequent to the event of man's "liberation" and accidentally but which was potentially present—though latent for a long time—as the reverse side of this liberation. It is characteristic of the basic relationship of modern man to reality that it was no longer the totality of human nature which was believed to link man with the universe, with God, with his fellow-men, and with all other existing entities, but reason alone. Man was thus primarily an individual ego-subject who by virtue of the light of reason possessed in his interiority the only infallible guide by means of which he could find his way to the certainty of an "external world." And all the forms of human community, such as the state, language, etc., were conceived as resulting from the common agreement of originally isolated individual subjects. Simultaneously, however, this evidence of his rational knowledge imparted to man the certainty of his claim to sovereign rulership over nature, a claim which was substantiated in the growth of modern technology. True enough, modern man is a lonely ruler: he does not live in an already established communal world but is compelled to create this communion by his own deeds, guided by his rational knowledge. The road which—after the breakdown of the medieval world order—led to the conquest of a new foundation of human existence, denotes thus a maximal increase in power, joined with a maximum of loneliness, and the entire history of modern times reflects repeated attempts to annul this loneliness. These attempts were aimed at the recapture of a vital human community, and they reached their apex in the philosophy of Hegel without, however, ever surrendering the basic idea that to be a thinking subject constitutes the essential definition of the nature of man.

Since it is without doubt the principal concern of present-day philosophy to overcome the "philosophy of subjectivity" and therewith to reverse a basic position which left its imprint on the entire modern age, we shall attempt to describe in the following pages the several stages of this development. The change can be diagnosed in some preparatory steps, along lines which often intertwine, and we shall confine our discussion to the two most important ones. The first starts out from that turning toward anthropology which occurred after the breakdown of German Idealism; the second leads by way of a further elaboration of the subject-object dichotomy in Husserl's Phenomenology to a point where it becomes evident that the question as to the nature of man and his relationship to being cannot be sufficiently clarified on the basis of the traditional concept of the subject.

The turn toward anthropology was characterized in the initial phase by the fact that, in place of Hegel's Absolute Spirit, man himself in his "concrete" sensori-somatic existence—rather than man as an "abstract" rational being—became the ultimate principle of philosophy. The nineteenth century tried to determine this concreteness in several different ways. The direction of these several ways toward "concrete man" is already indicated in Karl Marx's saying, "Man, that is the world of the human being." And these ways differ depending on the manner in which the "how" of "the world of the human being" is interpreted. For Marx himself and for Marxism it is the social conditions and relations which represent this "how"—conditions and relations within whose frame man produces the order which—by means of his work—satisfies his needs. The growing influence of the standpoint of the natural sciences, on the other hand, aided man in learning to understand "the world" as a biological problem, intimately related to the context of the *milieu,* that is, the "surrounding world" *(Umwelt)* or man's environment. The question as to the nature of man thus developed into the question as to the conditions under which this particular animal species with its corresponding endowment and equipment could existentially survive within a given environmental situation and by means of adaptation. "Life" thus became the maxim which was to elucidate the meaning of the looked-for concreteness of the human being, "life" understood in its dual sense—as a biological and as an historico-social phenomenon. While the latter position was elaborated in its purest form by Wilhelm Dilthey, Nietzsche's concept of life encompasses both factors, the historical and the biological.

The common denominator of all these endeavors lies in the fact that they were trying to interpret human life—whether more biologically or more historically oriented—from the point of view of pure *immanence,* that is, on the basis of a pretended absolute autonomy, as an ultimate "facticity" *(Tatsache) "hinter die nicht mehr zurückgegangen werden kann"* (behind which one cannot possibly retreat [Dilthey]); an ultimate which cannot find its ground and support in the metaphysics of some *"Hinterwelt"* (a world behind "this" world [Nietzsche]). We shall have to discuss later on how and why this concept of life in which the search for the "concrete" human being terminates, is itself determined by hidden metaphysical presuppositions and also why the forward thrust to this concept may be regarded as a final step in the consistent historical evolution of Western metaphysics.[10]

All these points of view can be detected as still active ingredients of present-day thinking. Arnold Gehlen's *Der Mensch* is a characteristic example of the perfected biological approach.[11] We begin our discussion with it because the strict consistency observed in this kind of approach offers the advantage that its limitations are clearly revealed by the intrinsic exigencies of the subject matter itself, without any special intent or effort on our part.

Gehlen delimits his interpretation of human nature on two sides: first, he marks it off against all attempts to understand man from a standpoint "beyond" the world (p. 12); second, against a biological interpretation which understands man as a mere "animal," which therefore sees him situated on the same plane with animalic being and at best grants him a higher layer of "soul" or "spirit," superimposed, as it were, on his animalic constitution. Gehlen thus takes as the guiding principle of his thesis the supposition that man must not be understood with a view to what he has in common with animals, and some subsequently superadded factor, but that all the factors which are efficaciously active in man, beginning with the lowest, purely organic ones, must from the outset be grasped in their specific significance (p. 14). It is, in Gehlen's opinion, precisely the equation of man and animal which renders a biological understanding of man impossible (p. 74). This latter can therefore have only an "anthropobiological" meaning (p. 8). And only as "anthropobiology" can the biological approach achieve its objective to comprehend man as a "design of nature" *(Naturentwurf) sui generis.* The anthropobiological question addressed to man relates therefore to the conditions of his existence. If one starts out by comparing man and animal, man must of necessity appear as an "underprivileged being" *(Mängelwesen).* The question must then read: how is this being, which cannot be compared with any of the known animals, capable of survival? In the case of the animal the vitality of survival is guaranteed by its adaptation to the given conditions of its environment: the surrounding world *(Umwelt)* and the specialization of individual organs and their functions are firmly ordered to one another, while for man there exists no such firm ordination. Man's mark of distinction is precisely his not-being-adapted, a condition which denotes free adaptability and world-overtness. All human functions, such as sensation, feeling, perception, language, derive from this their specific meaning, a meaning and significance which can in no way be compared with the role they play in animal life. These functions are not a simple actualization of a prior adaptation to a given environment. Our analysis will show that they are functions on which a living being which does not enjoy in an originary manner a firm correlation of environment and organic functions, must of necessity depend. They must therefore be understood as the "self-activated performance by virtue of which man transforms the privative existential conditions of an underprivileged being into the chances of his survival." Man, by virtue of his nature, must of necessity be an active being, and the quintessence and sum total of that nature which he transforms by his action into that which serves life, is the world of culture and civilization (p. 25 sq.). But in order to be able to act, man stands in need not only of a vista of possibilities but, in addition, of an actual independence of direct impulses; in short, the satisfaction of his needs and wants must be inhibited to some extent rather than being immediately fulfilled. Whereas in the animal sensation and reaction are directly interrelated, man owns the possibility of traversing the world in non-compulsive sensations (*triebfreien Empfindungen*) and of thus gaining a perspective of possibilities, of "world-over man" (p. 29). It is this capability of "retaining and restraining impulses" which brings to light man's "inwardness." All the sensori-motorial performances are not only carried out mechanically but with a self-awareness which moves them into the realm of cognition and makes them subject to control. Man must become conscious of himself in order to be able to survive as a human being. "He must acquire knowledge in order to become active; he must be active in order to stay alive tomorrow" (p. 40). Consciousness is thus understood as an auxiliary means of the organic process, and from this it follows that consciousness illumines in every instance just as much as is needed for an improvement of the life-process, that is, for a better endurance of existence. From this point of view Gehlen answers the question as to the reasons why man stands in need of language, imagination and other specific faculties (p. 57).

If then in this manner the actuality of consciousness is being "deduced" from the needs which an "underprivileged being" has in order to stay alive, it follows of necessity that all the diverse forms of man's intellectual and spiritual activity as a being conscious of himself may be regarded from the same point of view. The *Weltanschauung,* in the adoption of which the intellectual and spiritual activity of man terminates, is thus a guiding system which is necessitated by man's biological-anthropological condition (p. 51). In such a system man designs in a comprehensive manner the possibilities of those actions in which he must engage in order to survive. Man is a "highly cultivated being" (*Zuchtwesen* [p. 49]) who forms himself and his environment with a view to his survival.

It becomes evident at this point that the anthropological approach to the nature of man is unable to leave the track which was already implicitly delineated at the outset when this kind of approach posited as its goal the task of understanding man as a being that produces or creates itself. In the historical perspective, the positive significance of this approach lies in the fact that it was able to overcome the abstract conception of the subject. In doing this, it absorbed the entire wealth of natural-scientific knowledge and liberated such phenomena as sensation, speech, etc. from the one-sidedness of a purely natural-scientific questioning, on the one hand, and a purely humanistic intellectualism—and their supposed absolute autonomy—on the other. *The limitation,* however, of *the anthropological approach* is most clearly in evidence where it is most consistently adhered to. The boundary lines set by these limitations cannot be crossed at will but turn out to be those *blind alleys in which the process of man's taking absolute possession of himself*—a process that started with the advent of modern times—*terminated of necessity*. If consciousness is seen exclusively as an auxiliary means of the organic process—and on the basis of this kind of approach, which accepts life and its functions as ultimates, it cannot be seen otherwise—then consciousness can essentially be neither capable of nor destined for a recognition of that process itself. This was an idea of Schopenhauer's which in this context is being revived by Gehlen (p. 57). Consciousness can therefore not be capable of answering the question concerning the meaning of the life-process, simply because such an answer transcends the circumference of its functions. This meaning can only be indicated symbolically by saying it must be a "heightening of life" *(mehr an Leben),* in analogy to the manner in which Nietzsche saw it as a characteristic of life that it was striving for heights beyond itself, in the direction of the breeding of the over-man (p. 58).

If we ask, however, why the survival or the clinging-to-life and the heightening of life is to be regarded as a supreme value that casts light on the significance of all its functions, this question cannot be answered at all on the basis of the anthropological-biological approach. For this kind of questioning the naked "facticity" (that-ness; *das Dass*) of life remains an ultimate datum upon which man finds himself thrown back in his reflection. On this basis the question merely begets an insight into the meaninglessness of every "why." And yet, the question "why" was, after all, the aboriginal impulse of all philosophic thought. If therefore the anthropological-biological point of view is accepted as an ultimate criterion, the question "why" must be prohibited because its being-permitted would annul the very presupposition and premises of this approach. The fact that this narrow perspective cannot provide an ultimate criterion is substantiated by Gehlen himself in a more recent work which will be discussed later on.[12]

However, what becomes visible as the limitation of any attempt to base philosophic thought on anthropology—precisely if such an attempt is being pursued with consistency—can serve to illustrate the *situation of modern man:* its characteristic self-satisfied readiness to accept life in its striving for self-preservation and self-exaltation as an ultimate unquestioned and unquestionable fact. When translated from theory into practice, this assumption is believed to justify any amount of brutality in the struggle for naked self-preservation, whether it be of the individual, of a people, or of a state. But this satisfied complacency of thinking—which in most instances is completely ignorant of the consequences—remains unaware of the fact that it does not mark a scientifically established starting point for the question which man asks concerning his own self but is rather a sign and symptom of that wayless forlornness which Nietzsche described as one of the symptoms of European nihilism.[13] This kind of thinking, therefore, does not rise to a mode of self-reflection which would be capable of penetrating with its glance to the sources of the historically conditioned origin. For the interpretation of the force of conscious self-knowledge and self-understanding as a mere auxiliary function of some organic process is itself no more than an *interpretation (Deutung)* which is posited by man in his striving to understand himself within a set of definite, already established historical conditions.

The *aporia* to which Gehlen's approach leads us is thus indicative of the fact that the direction of our approach must be reversed: *instead of interpreting the self-understanding of man as a function of the facticity of life regarded as an ultimate, the interpretation of human existence*—as a kind of life which by its very constitution excludes the capacity of answering the question concerning its meaning—*must be understood as the function of a very specific manner of self-understanding*. For a certain kind and amount of self-understanding pertains inseparably to human existence, and this understanding is more than a powerless reflex of a static constitutional condition of this existence. In his self-understanding man designs a blueprint, as it were, of what he can be and should be, and in doing so he reaches out beyond everything that he has been. It is precisely when the problems implicit in the anthropological approach are consistently followed to their conclusions—as is being done in exemplary fashion in

Gehlen's treatise—that it becomes clearly evident why these problems *are not and cannot be narrowly self-confined* but point beyond themselves to a different plane, a plane upon which the approach to the phenomenon of man tries to derive its justification from the structure of human self-understanding.

This line of approach, running parallel with the anthropological-biological one, has never been broken since the breakdown of German Idealism. And in so far as it keeps in view man as that being who knows about himself and constantly maintains a certain understanding of himself, it is being directed—by the weight of the traditional tendency of modern times—toward an interpretation of man as ego-subject. This line of approach, therefore, remains initially within the frame of the epistemological subject-object dichotomy. We propose to show in the following pages how a new interpretation of the human being emerges, an interpretation in which also the former leaning of anthropology toward "concrete man" finds its fulfillment.

The impulses toward such a fulfillment have come—since the beginning of our century—from two sides: first of all, from *Wilhelm Dilthey* who—in contrast to the biological-naturalistic approach—comprehends the essence of "life" as that which is "known from within," that which reveals and manifests itself in the process of understanding, that is, as historical-social life. Since we shall have to discuss Dilthey in a different context,[14] it seems fitting to follow first the second line of development which begins with the *Phenomenology of Edmund Husserl.* Its situation in present day thought is very difficult to see with sufficient clarity, not only because Husserl's hitherto published writings—containing in their greater part only programmatic treatises—represent only a fraction of that which has become effective in the course of the elaboration of his program on the basis of lectures or other direct communications, but also and especially because Husserl's completed analyses have broken down the limiting confines as well as the self-interpretation implicit in his program, in a manner that remained concealed to Husserl himself. According to the program as it was stated in Husserl's *Ideas of a Pure Phenomenology* and later on in his *Cartesian Meditations* he meant his work to be a radicalization and completion of Descartes's demand to build all philosophic knowledge upon an absolutely certain insight that could withstand any doubts; to build it upon the self-evident certitude of the "I am—I think" and therewith to provide a firm ground for philosophy as a "strict science." [15]

However, supplementing and surpassing this programmatic self-interpretation, the historic significance of Husserl's work lies in the fact that precisely in his attempt to follow the ideas inherent in the modern subject-problem consistently to their conclusions, the points at which this problem is overcome and resolved come into view. And herewith a new foundation for the question concerning the nature of man is being laid. For it is precisely the limits within which—owing to Husserl's programmatic theses—this question remains enclosed in Husserl's own thinking as well as the contradiction between his "program" and that which is revealed unintentionally in his analyses, that make it possible for us to understand the further development of this question in the thinking of Max Scheler and its final form in the speculation of Martin Heidegger.

In the following pages, then, we shall begin with an account of the general fundamental features of Husserl's ideas, so that subsequently we may be able to show how on this basis the question concerning man is being asked and answered and what impelling motifs are contained in this answer.

The reduction of all cognition to the certitude of the "I think" does in Husserl's case not start out from an epistemological argument but is directed by a basic methodological conviction, the same conviction which was already acting as a guiding principle in his early mathematical and logical investigations. This conviction matured in the course of his encounter with the thesis of Positivism, according to which all experience must be reduced to that which is ultimately "given" and that all superimposed theories—deriving from traditional metaphysical and non-verifiable concepts—must be eliminated in order to arrive at *pure and originary experience*. From this demand for an originary experience in which "the things themselves" (*die Sachen selbst*) are brought into view without any distortion, Husserl was led to the question concerning the valid criteria of such an originary experience and concerning the tribunal that would be entitled to judge the originary nature of this kind of experience. And since "to experience" is a mode of "making-conscious-to-oneself" and of "retaining in one's consciousness," there can be no other tribunal than *consciousness itself with its experiences* which can mark and articulate the distinction between originary or authentic and unauthentic or merely imaginary experience. The one and only medium, however, through which we gain and have experience is *language*. And the "world" to which all experience is related is always an already linguistically interpreted world. Every entity is understood as a "this and that," as a thing named "thus or thus." This means that those inner perceptions *(Erlebnisse)* in which experience is gained have left their imprint in the expressions of language. Human speech can be original and authentic, a kind of speaking in which the intentional object is fully and truly present, or it may be non-original in the sense of being empty because the intentional object is not clearly and distinctly envisaged. To test or examine experience as to its originary character means thus above all to take the linguistic expressions as the starting point of an inquiry into the inner perceptions from which they derive their meaning and significance.

This method of inquiry was originally applied by Husserl to the concept of number, with the aim of "gaining clarity concerning the authentic originary and true meaning of the basic concepts of the doctrine of quantities and numbers by retrogression to the spontaneous activities of colligating and counting in which collections (such as totalities [*Inbgriffe*] or multiplicities [*Mengen*]) and quantities are given in an original-creative manner." [16] Soon, however, this kind of inquiry was related to all the objects of formal logic in general, to concepts, judgments, etc., and finally extended to the universal demand to apply *this retrospective inquiry into the inner experiences* in which an entity of such and such a nature is originally given "as itself" *(es selbst) to everything that can be meaningfully discussed,* whether it be a question of sense experience or of the highest problems of metaphysics. For every unauthentic utterance, every empty opinion, must refer to some original experience if its meaning is to become evident at all. The familiar every day phrase, "what is the meaning of what you say?" includes the demand not only for verbal clarification but also for an experiential demonstration of what is being said, a demonstration without which what is being said *(die Rede)* would remain meaningless.

The application of this method is known as *the phenomenological reduction:* it consists in tracing every entity back to the modes and operations of consciousness in which the entity is given as such in an originary manner. The phenomenological reduction makes it possible to describe that which is given exactly as it appears in consciousness, eliminating all meanings and intentions which transcend that which is given in consciousness. The phenomenological method is thus a comprehensive representation of consciousness and of those operations which make possible the givenness of entities. Consciousness, however, can be described and acts can be distinguished from one another only by virtue of the difference of their intentional objects, that is, by the difference of that of which I am conscious, by the difference of the directedness of acts toward their objects. The one and only theme, therefore, of the analysis of consciousness must be the differing modes of its directedness toward its object, and this being-directed is designated as the *intentionality* of consciousness. In this manner the question as to the nature or essence of everything which is, of everything that can be meaningfully discussed in human speech, is reduced to the question concerning the modes of consciousness, the modes of those inner experiences in which this nature or essence must appear in its originary quality. In this *return to the operations of consciousness* in which each and every entity is "constructed" as "this or that," it must become clearly evident what is meant by saying "this thing is" or "this thing is of such and such a quality or nature." Being and consciousness are thus *strictly correlated,* and there exists nothing—that is, nothing of which predications of any kind can be made—which does not require strictly corresponding constitutive operations of consciousness, operations in which the entity as such is given.

The essential differences that exist among all the possible objects of consciousness become thus the guiding principle *(Leitfaden)* in the retrogressive inquiry into the corresponding modes of consciousness. In this manner the phenomenological reduction—which began initially with the elimination of all preconceived opinions regarding all that which is *(das Seiende)*—acquires the significance of a *return to the ultimate absolute point* to which all the utterances concerning a "world" and concerning essential differences in the natures and structures of those entities which can be experientially perceived in this "world" must be referred, namely, the certitude which I have of myself as a being conscious of himself and of his world: the *Ego sum, ego cogito.* This certitude, however, does not have—as it does for Descartes—the significance of a first principle from which other principles can be deduced: it is for Husserl not the starting point of an epistemological argument but rather a *field of description.* The analyses of phenomenology move therefore constantly in a dual direction: they aim, on the one hand, at a "noematic" description, taking as its guide the essential differences among the species and regions of entities, while, on the other hand, they inquire correlatively into those operations of consciousness which correspond to these differences, operations in which the specific entities manifest themselves in their "givenness."

We have thus outlined the general frame within which *man* becomes the theme of Husserl's philosophy. Man is seen as a special kind of being, and as such he must, like every entity, become the principle of a constitutive retrogressive inquiry. Every human being knows himself as this particular individual, as a member of a particular nation or people, of a particular epoch, and so on. In whatever he is, man is determined by a specific mode of self-understanding, a self-understanding which is *a function of the operations of his consciousness.* This consciousness of himself makes man what he is. But herein precisely it becomes evident that the operations of human consciousness cannot be regarded as those of an isolated subject that enters in relation to others only owing to his consciousness. For what man is and what he understands himself to be as this particular individual, with this particular name and this particular personal destiny, that he is also with respect to his surrounding world (*Umwelt*). The role which he plays and the self-evaluation which he has of his role, he has not freely chosen; they have been dictated to him by the values which are already prevalent in his human surroundings. It is, however, due to the creative operations of his consciousness and to his self-understanding in his given situation that he is capable of playing his role, of meeting its challenges and of living more or less up to its exacting demands.

The given situation of a human being, reflected in his consciousness, as this specific "for-himself" and "for-others," thus presupposes the constitution of a world within which—in full self-understanding—he exists with others as this particular individual. However, in philosophic reflection man discovers himself as a center of intentional operations: he discovers himself in his consciousness, by virtue of which all entities are for him as they are, while he is for himself whatever he understands himself to be at any particular time. He is thus led back to this center of his self-confirmed certitude (*Selbstgewissheit*) as an "absolute" consciousness—absolute inasmuch as for his consciousness he himself as much as everything else is individualized and particularized. His self-understanding as an "I"—as "this particular human being"—is the product of intentional operations of his consciousness, in the reflective revelation of which he does not find himself as an isolated ego but as a human being in co-existence (*Miteinander*) with other human beings. This being-together-with-others, however, points—as far as its being-possible is concerned—once more to the operations of his consciousness, owing to which the others are present for him and with him in such a manner that he knows himself consciously together with them in a common world, a world in which the role in which he finds himself has been dictated or assigned to him by the community.

It would take us too far afield if we tried to discuss the problems which are encountered when the dual aspect of consciousness inherent in the method of phenomenological reduction is consistently pursued. On the other hand, it leads us to the source of all those "apperceptions" which form the basis of the givenness of all entities, including man in his self-perception, while on the other hand it leads us to a self-consciousness of man in the midst of an already given world, in co-existence with others. In our context it is of primary importance that we understand how, from which angle and within what boundaries the nature or essence of man is being envisaged in the perspective of Husserl's Phenomenology.

There is no doubt that from the very beginning Husserl's basic convictions had already delineated the way in which the principal question of metaphysics concerning the nature, the meaning, and the modes of being was to be answered. *Being* could accordingly and in principle only be understood *as a correlate of consciousness,* as a being-object for a consciousness in which an entity *sui generis* is given. The attitude of universal phenomenological reflection is therefore that of a *universal objectification,* that is, an objectification which understands all being exclusively as being-object. Although the absolute constitutive consciousness, the "I think" in its self-evident certitude, is ultimately an auto-generative stream of constitutive operations (a "stream of consciousness"), it can comprehend and reveal itself in its essence only in the *products* of its operations, that is, in the objective unities of the things themselves, and this revelation carries the meaning of *a demonstrable essential correlation between entities of every kind and the corresponding operations of consciousness*. That which actually forces its way to the fore and into experience as "this thing there" and necessitates an encounter, becomes thereby indifferent in the facticity of the givenness which determines its weight in human existence. It becomes an example of an entity of this particular kind and thus a guiding principle for the question as to which operations of consciousness pertain in unconditional universality and necessity to an entity of such a nature, an entity that can be "given" in this particular manner. The being of man, too, is to be understood in this way, namely, as the being of an object with respect to a consciousness which belongs to it by virtue of its essence. This kind of being then becomes the guiding principle for the inquiry into the hierarchical gradation of those apperceptions on the basis of which such an entity as "man in his particular situation" can become experientially accessible for himself as well as for others.

In this Cartesian regress to the "ego" as the ultimate starting point of all philosophic questions, there becomes then manifest an *inner ambivalence* precisely when this regress is carried out with radical consistency—an ambivalence of which Husserl himself was and remained unaware. But it remains at any rate his positive accomplishment that he developed the consequences of modern philosophy's start from the phenomenon of consciousness to the point where this starting principle was bound to reveal its inherent fallacy. It was precisely the methodological demand to demonstrate the "self-givenness" (*Selbstgegebenheit*) of all entities—as applied to the question concerning the nature of man—that provided the seed from which was to emerge in Heidegger's philosophy a decisive turning point of thought which led to the dissolution of the "philosophy of subjectivity." For Husserl's reductive regress to pure consciousness was *de facto* a reduction to a consciousness in which I take cognizance of myself as a solitary ego—a *solus ipse*—that is, the facticity of my own self in my historically conditioned situation. But it is precisely this "facticity" of my existence to which I am being led as the ultimate certitude and which in a different context was already foreshadowed in the concept of "life," which in the pursuance of the phenomenological method almost immediately eludes my grasp, owing to its being dissolved and reduced to those constitutive operations, on the basis of which I understand myself. In the phenomenological reflection I, as this particular human being, come into my view as an object of my consciousness. My factual existence, serving as an indifferent specimen to start with, becomes the guiding principle of the inquiry into those essential correlations, on the basis of which an entity of this kind can come within the field of consciousness. *This facticity of my existence as this particular individual in his specific historical situation is simply accepted without any further questioning.* Although this facticity is actually the "residual" of a phenomenological reduction to an ultimate and absolutely certain starting point, it does not come into view as such but rather serves immediately as the "leaping-off-point" (*Absprungspunkt*) to reach the "absolute ground" of universal reflection, that is, of a "detached contemplation" which questions all that which is (*alles Seiende*) concerning the operations of consciousness which have their source in this "absolute ground." And the place of the factual "I, this particular human being" is now giving way to a view of "consciousness in general" (*Bewusstsein überhaupt*). What remains obscure and hidden is the fact that every revelation of essential correlations between any individual entity and the corresponding operations of consciousness is nothing but an unveiling of those multiple possibilities in which this factual ego explicates itself within its historical horizon.

The repetition of the Cartesian beginning—and this is how Husserl understands his own philosophic endeavor—is thus more than a mere attempt on the part of a disciple of Descartes to win—after the demise of Hegelian metaphysics—

another belated victory for a philosophy that takes its start from the ego. The historical significance of Husserl's philosophy and its enduring dynamic force lie in its elasticity, indicative of the fact that in the present situation all philosophic reflection must start out from the absolute solitude of the isolated human being; that it must—by means of the phenomenological reduction—lead the philosopher back to the zero point of man's "absolute poverty;" and that, though this "poverty" aims beyond itself, this "beyond" is unattainable as long as the ego is held fast as the point of departure. And this incapacity of reaching out for that which transcends the zero point is indicated by the way in which Husserl himself interprets his thinking as a form of idealism, an idealism in which everything factual is reduced to the essential relations that prevail in the constitutive operations of consciousness. This interpretation, however, is in contradiction to the fact that all the possibilities of this constitutive analysis are already strictly delineated by the historical facticity of the starting point, that is, by those historical horizons within which the reflecting subject finds himself located and which themselves can therefore not be explained as products of the subject's active operation of his consciousness. Actually Husserl devoted extensive considerations to this historical situation of European man—as conditioned by the *factum* of science and of the scientific interpretation of the world—in his final philosophic investigations, especially in the treatise which deals with the Crisis of European Science and Transcendental Phenomenology.[17] He demonstrated in this treatise that in the last analysis he was not so much interested in the general "essence" (*Wesen*) of man and human consciousness in general but rather in the particular human individual in his particular historical situation, in his possibilties, his needs and his predicaments.

The boundaries within which Husserl formulated the question concerning the nature of man were transcended in two directions: (1) by *Max Scheler,* who raised the objection that the being-human of man cannot be understood as a being-object for a constitutive consciousness; and (2) by *Martin Heidegger,* for whom man in his historical facticity —which, though partly hidden, was already in Husserl's thinking the efficient force—is now quite manifestly placed in the center of the questioning, a questioning, however, which subsequently reaches out beyond man and unfolds the problem of man within the horizon of the question concerning the nature of being.

In the following brief account of the thinking of Max Scheler [18] we must disregard the fact that his philosophic development is divided into several epochs which are characterized by changes in his metaphysical position. This development leads from an originally personal concept of God to the idea of an original existing entity, split into the duality of "spirit" (*Geist*) and "drive" (*Drang*). If one confronts his utterances from different periods of his philosophic development with one another, one is bound to find in them some contradictory statements and conclusions. In our context, however, it is merely a question of making visible in its inner consequences the basic trend in Scheler's thought, which persists with unbroken continuity from his first phenomenological beginnings to the metaphysics embedded in his last works.

Whereas for Husserl—owing to his methodological convictions—the human person presented only *one* problem of the constitution of consciousness among others, for Scheler the question concerning the nature of personal being occupies a central position from the outset. Scheler's conviction that being-person differs essentially from being-object, results immediately in a definition of the nature of consciousness and its acts which deviates from Husserl's definition. The acts as constitutive operations cannot be exhaustively characterized by their "essential content" (*Gehaltwesen*), by their intentional relationship to something, but are according to their being wholly "execution" (*Vollzug*) and cannot in their essence become objects, not even by means of reflection: "The facticity of reflection differs altogether from any representational attitude." [19] "It pertains to the essence of the being of acts that they are experienced only in their execution and that they are given in reflection."[20] If then in the analysis of intentionality acts of many different kinds can be distinguished, the central question arises: "which executor 'belongs' essentially to the execution of all these different kinds of acts?[21] This executor is designated as *person.* And it is thus the person who makes possible the unity of all acts in one and the same consciousness. This person is no object, no substantial unity, and it cannot therefore—as was the case in Husserl's speculation—be understood as the personality of man in the world, as a constitutive product, as some or any kind of objectivity; the person "is" or "exists" only in the execution of the act and is therefore nothing but a being that executes acts.

With this thesis Scheler has crossed a boundary which we met in Husserl's analysis of man and which is anchored in Husserl's doctrine of reflection. For Husserl the acts, too—as objectified in reflection—become the guiding principle of a constitutive analysis, which manifests its formation in consciousness in the form of "units of endurance" (*Einheiten der Dauer*).[22] For Scheler, on the other hand, who abandoned this *identification of being and being-object,* the way was free to proceed to the problems of human existence, problems which in turn in Heidegger's philosophy were to lead to the idea of *Existenz.* Scheler, however, did not proceed any further in this direction but, guided by the premises of his starting point, arrived at entirely different conclusions. He asked: how then are we to understand the nature of man in his metaphysical significance? The notion of "person" is made clear and distinct by being related to the idea of "spirit" (*Geist*). For Scheler "spirit" denotes everything "that is of the nature of act, intentionality, and fulfillment of meaning." A person is "the essential, necessary, and unique form in which 'spirit'—provided it is a question of concrete spirit—exists."[23]

With this definition Scheler seeks to overcome the tradition of idealism, remnants of which were still alive in Husserl's concept of subjectivity. According to this tradition, the highest principle—that is, the Absolute—was expressed in the equation spirit-thought-reason (*Vernunft*). The principle of the unity of all executed acts which makes the person a person is neither intellect nor will. "All these distinctions express . . . only certain abstract features of that concrete personal act" [24] which as such is more than this sum total. The inner core which is found in the person may be defined as follows: Spirit is primarily the *capacity of taking hold of pure thusness* (*So-sein*), of pure essences; spirit is "a being-determinable by the thusness of things themselves." [25] The correlate of the acts of the spirit (*geistige Akte*) is a world of pure thusness, and it is in the execution of these acts that man attains to true being (nature, essence). Scheler—deviating from Husserl—thus interprets the phenomenological reduction as a reduction to the contemplatively envisaged essences. It is the capacity of gaining a purely contemplative attitude, an attitude which renounces the life-urge (*Lebensdrang*). And it is only by virtue of this capacity to posit and perform such spiritual acts that man differs essentially from the animal, whereas his intellect sets him apart from the animal only in degree but not in kind. According to Scheler, it is the intellect which characterizes man as *homo faber,* as a being who uses knowledge as a tool, a being who attains to his perfection in the development of the natural sciences and their application. As a "spiritual being" (*Geistwesen*), on the other hand, man is the one who can negate (*der Neinsagenkönner*), the ascetic of life, who alone among all entities can be prompted to ask the question: "Why, after all, is there a world? Why and how am I?" [26]

In its capacity of negation (of "saying-no") the spirit is simultaneously the power which makes it possible for entities to become and be themselves. It is not a specific property (*Eigenart*) of man which he has at his disposal but "an attribute of entities themselves which becomes manifest in man, in the concentrated unity of the self-collected person. The spirit as such, however, is in its 'pure' form originally without any 'power,' 'energy' (*Kraft*) and 'activity.'"[27] The vivification or vitalization of the spirit is brought about only "by the interpenetration of the originally powerless spirit and the originally demonic drive—a drive which is originally blind with respect to all spiritual ideas and values—that is, by the growing ideation and spiritualization of those painful hardships which are oppressively alive behind the images of things."[27a] "The spirit ideates life. But it is life alone which is capable of setting the spirit in active motion and of actualizing it."[28] And the spirit must make use of the urges and drives in order to attain to its realization. The actual realizations that are achieved at any given time—realizations in which this struggle between spirit and drive is being fought—becomes thus philosophically relevant.

This theory—no matter how many traditional features it may contain or how dubitable it may be—fulfilled for Scheler the function of leading him toward the entire plenitude of the possible empirical knowledge about man. He absorbed and appropriated Nietzsche's theory of *ressentiment,* the discoveries of sociology, of environmental research, and of depth psychology. "By acquiring, step by step, the insight that concrete human reality is something which is metaphysically relevant, he gained the legitimation to delve into this reality.[29] This integration of particularized empirical knowledge in the structural whole of a unified metaphysics constitutes the great suggestive force which emanates from Scheler's writings. It was possible for him to achieve this integration because he understood man as that kind of being in whom the world process of the sublimation of the drive toward spirit is consummated. Man is described by Scheler as a microcosm, but he gives a new interpretation of that ancient doctrine. Man is a microcosm because in him unfolds the metaphysical dramatic conflict between spirit and drive, a drama in which "that which is" (*das Seiende*) attains to self-knowledge. And thus it is "on the basis of the image of the human essence—the object of philosophico-anthropological research—that . . . conclusions can be drawn concerning the true attributes of the supreme and ultimate ground of all things." [30] For this process of man's incarnation (*Menschwerdung*) in consequence of the sublimation of the drive—a sublimation which reveals man as the ascetic of life—and man's elevation to a plane where he is able to contemplate pure essences, is simultaneously the process of man's divinization (*Gottwerdung*): "The aboriginal Existent (*das Urseiende*) acquires self-consciousness in man, in the very same act in which man grounds himself and contemplates himself in that Existent." [31] Man as the "meeting-place" (*Treffpunkt*) of spirit and drive is thus the unique *locus* of the self-realization of God.[32] And it is the task of humanity to actualize this precarious balance between spirit and drive, to combine the Asiatic psychotechnical practice of world-renunciation with the Western idea of technological world domination in a loving rapture that terminates in the contemplation of pure essences.[33]

And so we see that there persists in Scheler a consistent pattern of thought, from his early beginnings—which were determined by the problems of Husserl's phenomenology of consciousness—to his final metaphysical speculation. One of the motifs that were efficacious in Husserl's Phenomenology, viz., the contemplation of pure essences, has become an integral part of Scheler's metaphysics of man, a metaphysics which terminates in the end in a dualistic conception of the original ground of all that which is *(Urgrund des Seienden).* The antagonism between "spirit" and "life" recurs in Scheler —an antagonism which was predominant among the problems of nineteenth century philosophy ever since Hegel's death and which has found a final exaggerated formulation in *Ludwig Klages,* who deviates grossly from the original meaning of these two concepts. The concept of "life" owed its origin to the attempt to penetrate from the "abstract" concept of a rational subject to the "concrete" human being, but the philosophy of the nineteenth century saw no possibility of understanding this re-actively gained concept in any other way than in radical opposition to the concept of "spirit." This opposition—recurring within the frame of reference of Scheler's thinking as the opposition between "spirit" and "drive" was utilized by Scheler not only for the purpose of elaborating a "concrete" philosophy of man but as a springboard for the development of his "metanthropology," [34] that is, a metaphysics which is founded upon a philosophy of man which has absorbed every kind of empirical knowledge about man. In this kind of thinking the return of philosophy—which since Hegel's death circled about man, intending to establish anthropology as the basic philosophic discipline—to metaphysics has thus been consummated in an exemplary manner; in addition, *one* of the possibilities inherent in Husserl's starting point has been brought to fruition. It will become clear in pursuing the way from Husserl to Heidegger's definition of the essence of man that Scheler actualized indeed only *one* such possibility, while another one was lost sight of in the process. We will then be faced with the decision as to whether both ways (that of Husserl and that of Heidegger) present equally viable possibilities or whether what takes place in Heidegger's thinking is perhaps a radicalization of the problem of man which leads even more deeply into the center of human self-understanding.

We have seen that the methodological point of departure is determined by a tension *(Spannung)* relating (1) to the reduction of the absolute *Ego cogito* which as the ego of the solitary reflecting subject represents an ultimate no longer questioned *factum;* and (2) to the "leaping" *(Absprung)* from this *factum* into the attitude of a "disinterested" or "detached" spectator, to whom everything factual reveals itself as a realization of essential relationships. This latter idea was led to its terminal conclusion by Scheler. Metaphysically considered, man in his historically conditioned facticity is the *locus*—a *locus* that remains indifferent in its facticity—where the drama unfolds within the dualistically split "aboriginal existent" (*das Urseiende*) is being staged. The schema of this explication of the world is basically teleological: the world-process is so designed that—by means of the spirit's integration in a world determined by drive—the pure relations among essences are brought to light. The drive itself, as a kind of demiurge, is supposed to provide the necessary driving energies. Even though in this schema the present historical situation with its task of exercising a balancing function is assigned its fitting place, the meaning of this teleological interpretation is not seen in a *deeper immersion* in this situation but rather in the *victorious emergence* from it, in a process which in the philosopher's mind reveals already this final egress. If, however, the most profound characteristic of the historically conditioned facticity is the incertitude regarding the future, the naked *factum* of "standing" in this particular situation—a stance which cannot in advance be sure of any "whither"—then there is no doubt that in this as in any other kind of teleological ordination this specific characteristic, which expresses the fundamental inner experience *(das Grunderlebnis)* of our time, has been suppressed. And the same is true of Husserl's interpretation of the teleology of the development of the West, a development which is supposed to be oriented toward reason *(Vernunft)*. But because, on the other hand, within the frame of Husserl's thinking the fact that the "I think"—as the supposed "absolute" starting point of philosophic reflection—is nothing but the Ego of actual man, embedded in his actual historical situation, remains latently efficacious as a disquieting ingredient, Scheler's teleological metaphysics was designed to alleviate this disquietude. And this precisely is the point at which the further development of Phenomenology toward the "existential ontology" *(Existenzial-Ontologie)* of Heidegger begins.

Heidegger's thinking, however, is by no means to be understood exclusively as further development of Husserlian motifs. The question as to all the factors of the philosophic tradition which determine in great measure Heidegger's thinking could be answered only by a synoptic view of his work in its entirety. Such a view, however, is not possible as yet. We are therefore in our context chiefly concerned with the meaning of the radicalization of the question as to the nature of man, in the progression from Husserl and Scheler to Heidegger. With regard to this question, the meaning of Heidegger's relationship to Husserl seems to be that only in Heidegger's philosophy the historical and existential presuppositions become visible which made it possible to use Phenomenology as a method of reduction.[35] This means that *the final completion and radicalization of Descartes's point of departure—as embodied in Husserl's Phenomenology and as confirmed by Husserl's own evaluation of his philosophy—brings simultaneously to light the problematic nature and the inherent weakness of the ground of modern thought laid by Descartes, so much so that Heidegger was able to make this weakness his own point of departure.*

In the work of Scheler we found the insight that reflection does not mean objectification, that the nature of the acts of the subject can become accessible only in their execution and not as objects. Herewith Husserl's equation of being and being-object had already shown itself demonstrably insufficient for the comprehension of the nature or essence of the subject. However, within the frame of Scheler's metaphysics of an "intuition of essences" *(Wesenserschauung)* this insight could not become efficacious in its full range and significance. Heidegger went further in posing explicitly *the question concerning the subjectivity of the subject* and concerning the meaning of the execution of acts.[36] The traditional definition of man as an ego-subject is therewith abandoned and the question concerning the nature of man is shifted to a greater depth. The question now reads: is the assertion true at all that human existence *(Dasein)* can be exhaustively defined as an ego-subject that finds himself confronted with a world of objects? The fact is that modern philosophy has analyzed the *cogitare* of the ego within certain limits, but it has completely neglected to discuss the nature of the *sum*.[37] Modern philosophy has thus understood the being of man in the same sense as the being of other "objects" and has failed to see that being-man means something fundamentally different. It has overlooked the fact that man is the only entity which in its being is concerned with its own being. This and nothing else is meant when Heidegger says that *care* or *concern (Sorge)* constitutes the fundamental structure of human existence. The highest possibility of human *Dasein* is therefore not a theoretical gaining of distance *(das Abstandgewinnen)* whereby my always *very own* existence in its empirico-historical actuality is validated only as the realization of a universal "essence of man," but this highest human possibility is rather the resolute appropriation of this facticity, into which the human essence has been "thrown" (*geworfen*). The world [38] can then no longer be understood as the product of the constitutive operations of the subject but as that wherein human *Dasein* always finds itself and which hands to it the amplitude of all its possibilities of existing, of gaining itself qua Self, or of losing itself. This losing-itself may assume the mode of a surrender or a being handed over to the "public," to *das Man* (the one-like-many, the public ego), to that which is so general and impersonal that man is no longer himself, no longer a Self. It is this "average level" *(Durchschnittlichkeit)* of man's everyday existence—wherein he receives the directives for his behavior by his fellow-men and their opinions and prejudices, from which the question concerning the nature of man must start out. This has nothing to do with a mere "critique of the spirit of the age" *(Zeitkritik)* but rather serves to reveal one of the fundamental structural designs of human *Dasein*. And since human *Dasein* is that kind of entity which in its being is concerned about its being, all such predications concerning man do not only state some actual and essential facticity but imply already an *assault* upon man as such. This means that the analysis of the structure of human *Dasein* has its *locus* beyond the traditional distinction between theoretical and practical philosophy. For every amount of clarifying self-analysis on the part of man implies already a certain change in man himself. Even though he may not behave in accordance with the greater lucidity he has gained, even though he may not draw any conclusions from it with respect to his actions, his behavior is nonetheless no longer the same: it may, negatively, be characterized by his closing himself to a potentiality which was revealed to him in the clarifying introspection. Human *Dasein* is therefore essentially characterized by the fact that man finds himself within an amplitude of possibilities which have been handed to him by his personal destiny *(Geschick)*. However, as we may conclude from what we have just said, possibility or potentiality does not mean in this case something which is simply being stated as likely to happen if certain conditions are given. The potentialities of man are that to which he is forever related or proportioned, that concerning which he has already made his decision by either losing or finding and gaining himself. Even in losing himself man remains concerned about himself when he uses every possible excuse to save himself and secure himself in view of the "call of conscience" which warns him not simply to accept *das Man* as the guide of his actions but to exist "authentically," that is, to exist "as himself."

The nature of care *(Sorge)* becomes most articulate whenever—in *"Angst"* (dread)—all of man's simply given matter-of-course possibilities become questionable. This *Angst* is at bottom an anxiety concerning himself. It is therefore unlike the "fear" *(Furcht)* of definite dangers which threaten from the world. *Angst* calls in question man's *Dasein* as a whole. But for this very reason, only *Angst* can impart to man the "resoluteness" *(Entschlossenheit)* to choose his very own possibilities. Only in view of the possibility of the not-being of his own self can man acquire the freedom of finding and choosing himself. Human *Dasein* is therefore essentially defined as 'being-unto-death" *(Sein zum Tode),* and it reveals itself in its internal structure as "finite." *Finitude* does not enunciate the fact that "all men are mortal" but rather that all the possibilities which man "possesses" are determined by the situation into which he is placed by his destiny *(geschickhaft)* from the very beginning. Finitude is indicative of the facticity of human *Dasein,* a facticity which acquires its most expressive profile in man's confrontation with *death,* that is, with the annihilation of all human possibilities.

Heidegger's analysis of the fundamental structures of human *Dasein* has often been misunderstood. It has been called an expression of a gloomy philosophy of death, and it has been objected that Heidegger's concept of man is unduly weighted by a preconceived perspective which sees only the dark side of human *Dasein.* In view of these misinterpretations it should be emphasized that the elaboration of the finiteness of *Dasein* in its facticity represents *a radical attack on the entire Western tradition of human self-understanding.* Ever since Plato the essence of man was construed as a supra-historical potentiality and the *factum* of each particular human *Dasein* in its historical individuality was interpreted with a view to this supra-historical frame of reference *(Bezugspunkt).* Individual man in his historically conditioned facticity and uniqueness thus saw himself as a mere actualization of the constant potentiality of the human essence, and he believed that—in view of the innate potentialities of his essence—it was possible for him to be liberated from his facticity. The significance of the radical change brought about by Heidegger's thinking may be stated as follows: the *factum* of man as an individual as well as the *factum* of an historical epoch are no longer understood with a view to the universal and constant potentialities inherent in the human essence but, conversely, the facticity of the always personalized individual human *Dasein* as well as the facticity of each and every historical epoch are seen as the amplitude within which the potentialities of being-human can be discussed at all. This is what Heidegger means when he says that the "essence" *(das Wesen)* of *Dasein* lies in its existence.[39]

That "being-thrown-back" to the always individual subjectivity of the ego—which from Descartes to Husserl marked the starting point of the philosophic questioning and which impressed upon modern philosophy the character of an ego-philosophy—becomes now the main theme precisely in the hitherto neglected character of its facticity. It thus becomes evident that this traditional form of philosophy and the kind of human self-understanding of which modern philosophy is an articulate expression, represents only one particular mode of how man in a specific historical situation relates himself to his existence. This particular mode is characterized by the fact that here man is forgetful of the fundamental nature of his existence and—in the face of insecurity and uncertainty—allows himself to succumb to the rule of a "concern for certitude" *(Sorge der Gewissheit).* By permitting this to happen, he seeks to overcome—by means of the autonomous appropriation of certain rules of reason—the danger, more intensely experienced since Descartes, which threatens a human being who can no longer trustingly believe in a divine Providence. It is the significance of Heidegger's critical labors to have demasked the fallacy which consists in trying to found human *Dasein* upon scientific certitude. Heidegger has demonstrated that this attempt leads to a mere illusory certitude, that it signalizes a flight into insights which, to be sure, are universally valid but which, precisely because of their *universal* validity, remain non-obligatory for the *individual.* Heidegger thus continues the line of thought which had long been at work as an undercurrent and as a counter-movement against the ideal of certitude which dominated modern philosophy. This undercurrent becomes visible on the surface only occasionally, as happened, for example, in the thinking of Pascal and Kierkegaard. Heidegger—in critically attacking the traditional attempts to interpret the nature of man by viewing it in relation to his "constant essence"—makes, first of all, visible the point of departure of this trend of modern philosophy, and he shows that this road had ended in a blind alley. The reduction of all these beginnings to that which lies behind them as a compelling force—that is, the reduction to the one and only certitude of the naked *factum (das Dass)* of human existence—can itself be understood as being indicative of this particular historical situation, a situation in which man has become fully aware of the loss of his anchorage in some universally binding acknowledged system of norms and values and the corresponding and correlative institutions.

What we have said in the preceding pages may suffice to characterize the new horizon within which Heidegger moves in *"Being and Time"* (1927).[40] In this new beginning, several different avenues seemed to be left open, especially since up to now only the first part of this work has been published. In what manner some of these open possibilities were interpreted is shown by the way in which *French* philosophy developed Heidegger's ideas.[41]

For *Jean-Paul Sartre,* too, it is the facticity of human *Dasein* which, having been "thrown" into a non-transparent opaque world, provides the foundation in which *Dasein* tries to "ground" itself and gain hold of itself. But whereas for Heidegger this analysis of *Dasein* fulfilled only the function of a "fundamental ontology" which was to prepare the ground for the philosophic inquiry into the nature of being, Sartre comes forward with a very definite answer: man is said to be separated from "being-in-itself" *(l'être-en-soi),* that is, from the "absolute," by an abyss. This abyss, however, is not indicative of a distance between one individual and another; man himself is the abyss: man himself is that being through whom nothingness or the naught comes into the world. This means that man himself is the gaping hole of the naught: his "being-for-himself" *(l'être pour-soi)* can never attain "being-in-itself" *(l'en-soi).* And why not? Because to reach being-in-itself he would have to be self-identical. But man is always what he is not yet, and he is never what he already is. And thus man can never be "fixed" in his essence: his existence is essentially a "being-beside-himself," an ek-static being, and all the definitions which he is trying to give of himself must of necessity fall short of his existence. He is never determinable by the "having" of certain qualities, by the constitutive elements of his past: he rather makes and remakes himself again and again, to become what he then retrospectively "is." Man's facticity is furthermore determined by the fact that *he lays and is his own ground,* that he always decides or chooses in a "groundless" decision because every "grounding" of a decision by previously conceived intentions, by tradition, etc., would immediately destroy his [absolute] freedom. For the reality of man, therefore, being is confined to action.[42] In the series of novels titled *The Ways of Freedom,* especially in the first volume ("The Time of Ripeness"), this struggle of man for his self-affirmation in freedom is vividly presented.

We meet then in Sartre's thinking with a paradoxical effect of Heidegger's premises: starting out from some of Heidegger's ideas concerning the necessary reversal of that trend of modern thought which aimed at the realization of the boundless freedom and autonomy of man, Sartre and his followers develop a philosophy which carries this modern movement to its highest peaks, in an attempt to bring to life a totally emancipated human being who, having discovered his [absolute] freedom, "has no longer any need of the gods." [43] Nietzsche's idea of the man who has been raised to the stature of the Superman is here echoed and even surpassed. According to Sartre, it is only in the certitude of possessing a boundless and groundless freedom that man can gain an attitude which makes it possible for him to form his world, an attitude which implies an obligation to act without asking for a "why" of the action, simply because the action is itself the reason for every "why."

It is precisely this "groundlessness"—the absence of any reason or "ground" for human actions—which caused *Albert Camus* to describe human existence as irremediably absurd. *The Myth of Sisyphus* and *The Plague* present men who do not know why they fulfill their daily obligations but who fulfill them nevertheless. Any reasons for human actions which derive from sanctions rooted in a firm hierarchy of values are termed illusory. Nor is man capable of positing a new order of values. He has, however, an acute consciousness of deprivation, a consciousness which is no longer—as in the thinking of Sartre—covered up by man's supposed absolute autonomy which would allow him to posit himself as the absolute ground. This emphasis on *the absurdity of human exist-*

ence in its facticity signifies the reduction of the problem to a point where it becomes clearly manifest that the attempt to ground human existence upon itself cannot succeed and that, though the road toward the attainment of any ground cannot bypass human existence, it cannot terminate in human existence as if it were an ultimate absolute. And thus we see here once more, from a different perspective, the tendency of present-day thinking to overcome a purely anthropological foundation of philosophy. This overcoming does not again lead us into a realm of intuited pure and constant essences but takes its start from the growing acuteness of the problems posed by facticity, in consonance with the initial steps taken by Heidegger in *Being and Time*. These steps set the stage for an inquiry into the nature (or essence) of man which leaves behind the "existentialism" of Sartre.

In Heidegger's later writings [44] it becomes clear that the problems initially discussed in *Being and Time* are further developed in a direction diametrically opposed to the thinking of Sartre. The term existence does not (as it does in Sartre) refer to man as an entity which, owing to the gaping hole of nothingness which is lodged within man himself, is separated from being, but existence, conceived as the fundamental determination of man is now understood as *"Ek-sistenz"* (ex-sistence), as a "standing-out" beyond the individual self, as the potentiality of "being-open," of overtness for being. The earlier analyses of Heidegger which were aimed at the creation of a fundamental ontology are by no means annulled or revoked. But whereas the concepts which were used in *Being and Time* to interpret the fundamental structures of human *Dasein*—such as authenticity and non-authenticity, resolution in the face of the certainty of death etc.—remain formally inarticulated in the earlier work, so that nothing can be predicated concerning that content which effectuates the acquisition of an authentic self, they now acquire a fulfilled content in the interpretation of the potentiality of existence as "overtness for being," as the capacity of listening to the language of being.[45] Man is therefore the place where—in the medium of language—the "clearing" *(Lichtung)* of being occurs. The speaking about being is not an act in which man asserts and assumes "absolute autonomy" *(Selbstbemächtigung),* but being manifests itself in speaking, above all in the speech and the words of poets and thinkers, and man's attitude is that of listening and understanding. It is no longer in the power of man to effectuate the clearing of being or to live in "separation from being" *(Seinsferne),* but it is the destiny of being itself to provide the possibility for man to live either in separation from or in the vicinity of being. In short, man is not the lord and master of being but, as the "shepherd of being," he stands in the service of being.

Heidegger uses great care in choosing formulations which avoid any hard and fast fixation of the notion of being and which are only aimed at calling attention to the position of man and to the meaning of his language. In doing this, he touches on the idea of a history of being which would serve to reaffirm that separation from being and nearness to being are not possibilities which man can actualize at will but are a historically conditioned destiny. In that way the interconnection between being and the facticity of human *Dasein* is given a more profound causal explication, and the "historicity" (*Geschichtlichkeit*) of man is being anchored in the destiny *(Geschick)* of being.

As far as the "Christian existentialism," developed in *France,* is concerned, there is likewise to be found a countermovement against Sartre's "atheistic existentialism" [46] but simultaneously also a turning away from the field of historicity and its facticity. French Christian existentialism, too, is centered in the free act of human existence, but this act in its freedom and with respect to its potentialities is not grounded in man himself but is free only to the extent that it is a participation in that "absolute act" which is equated with being and with God: it is a participation in that love wherein man realizes the freedom of his essence. Freedom is thus not, as in the case of Sartre, a "nihilation" *(Nichtigwerden)* of being in order to enable man to re-create it in absolute autonomy *(selbstmächtig),* but freedom is the transition from nothingness to being. It is a received freedom, freedom as a mandate. In this formal schema we can discern a relationship with that basic tendency of Heidegger which aims at the overcoming of the idea of an absolutely autonomous human being. The essential difference lies in the fact that French Christian existentialism equates being with God and sees the modes of existing as essential potentialities of man, not as historically conditioned aspects of the individual human destiny.

Opposed to all this is the idea of man embodied in the thinking of *Karl Jaspers.* Notwithstanding the fact that he agrees with Heidegger in turning against a concept of philosophy which regards it as an objective science that imparts to man certainty by virtue of the power of knowledge, his notion of existence lacks completely the element of historicity, understood as a tie which binds man to his unique and unrepeatable situation, a situation which itself derives from the history of being. Human existence in its fundamental structures—which is said to become most lucid in its "limit-situations" *(Grenzsituationen)*—is destined to suffer "shipwreck" *(das Scheitern)* and is supposed to gain hold of itself only in shipwreck. "Suffering shipwreck," however, does not condemn existence to absurdity but points the way to *faith.* All entities that are appropriated by human knowledge, that are formed by art, that are actualized in the personal existence of man, are so many "ciphers" *(Chiffres)* for a "transcendence" which must not be merely intellectually accepted but must be tested by the total commitment of personal existence in order to disclose its meaning to [philosophic] faith.

In the unfolding inquiry into the nature of man the writings of *Hans Lipps* occupy a special hitherto not sufficiently appreciated position, chiefly because of their more or less aphoristic character. Since they do not aim at a plainly recognizable systematic synthesis, they cannot be simply fitted into one of the previously discussed trends of thought but are characterized by a very independent elaboration of certain suggestions which the author has received from Husserl and

Heidegger. The center of his thinking is occupied by the question concerning the original and immediate world-relationship of man, the interpretation of which led Lipps already in his earliest treatise [47] to a critical encounter with the analysis of this relationship from the point of view of psychology and the phenomenology of consciousness, on the basis of the concept of intentionality. He has thus taken over from his teacher Husserl the tendency toward phenomenological description but not Husserl's analytic method of intentionality. The immediate "having" of the world in sensory experience must not be misunderstood as a relationship of consciousness to things as objects of intentionality.[48] Lipps rather contends that the senses exercise their original function in dealing with things, in "handling" things. What is meant by a "thing" cannot be explained by having recourse to the aprioristic laws of consciousness, to the pure concepts of reason—which always presupposes the projection of the logical structure of an *ens praedicabile* into the thing-structure—but rather by the disclosure of the always predominating "anticipation of attitudes" (*Einstellungen*).[49] These attitudes are more than anticipations of possible knowledge because they presuppose man's self-understanding of the potentialities of his *Dasein*. With these ideas Lipps had initiated the critique of the subject-object problem in modern philosophy even prior to the publication of Heidegger's *Being and Time*. He had actually already taken the decisive step from a phenomenological analysis of consciousness to an interpretation of man's antecedent being-in-the-world, and he was therefore in a position to find in the work of Heidegger a confirmation of his own thinking, which he himself interpreted as a "philosophy of existence." However, Lipps reaches out beyond the thematic structure of Heidegger's work by integrating in his existential analysis the question as to the nature of sensory experience (*Empfinden*) and its function in the exploration of nature; he demonstrates that the concept of nature in the physical and biological sciences does not coincide with the kind of immediate experience which man has of nature in his constitution as a "natural being" *(Naturwesen)*.[50] Hand in hand with this argument goes the elaboration of the role—only briefly touched upon by Heidegger—which logic plays in such a "hermeneutic philosophy" [51] which interprets *Dasein* in its self-understanding. The unconditionally universal apriori of human nature which such a philosophy has to elucidate is grounded more deeply than those aprioristic structures and concepts which are embedded in the self-reflecting consciousness, and the disclosure of this universal apriori makes it possible to limit the amplitude of the epistemological relationship to objects and the corresponding logic of predication.

The preceding paragraphs have attempted to explain the meaning of the decisive change in present day philosophy: *the overcoming of the basically anthropological approach by a reduction of the inquiry into the nature of man to the question of human existence*. The turning away from the definition of man as an isolated ego-subject does no longer permit us to speak of man as a subject in opposition to the world. We are henceforth compelled to understand the problem of the world in unison with the problem of man. The inquiry into the meaning of the concept "world" is therefore our next task.

CHAPTER II

The World-Concept

A survey of the main themes of philosophy in the second half of the nineteenth and into the beginning of the twentieth century reveals that among these themes the concept of the "world"—which at one time, under the title "cosmology," was one of the disciplines subsumed under the heading *Metaphysica specialis*—plays practically no part. The reason lies in the fact that a certain concept of "world" had been accepted as so self-evident and exclusively valid that its explicit thematic discussion was considered unnecessary. The problems of the "world" with which the contemporary philosophic discussion is preoccupied presupposes that this naive confidence has been shaken, and therewith a long forgotten realm of problems has once again become an integral part of philosophy. In the following pages we shall attempt to give an account of *the road which present day thinking has been following, starting out from the traditional and self-evident concept of the "world" and arriving at a re-definition of the nature of the world, owing to the fact that this supposed self-evidence was radically called in question.*

Now this changed concept of the world is by no means the exclusive concern of philosophy. The latter makes only explicit what was already implicitly or latently at work—as a change in the relationship of man to the "world"—in both the pre-scientific and the scientific development. We must therefore distinguish the *explicit* philosophic discussion of the world-problem from its *implicit* discussion. The latter represents a novel clarification of the world-problem as it followed—more or less independently from the contemporaneous philosophic teaching—especially in the fields of biology and psychology, and it did so solely under the impetus of the particular problems posed by these disciplines. Even though our own presentation has as its theme primarily the development of the *explicit philosophic* elaboration of the world-problem, we shall nonetheless—in order to understand the meaning and significance of this development—have to refer also to the *implicit* contributions which have accrued from the investigations carried on by those individual scientific disciplines which have aided in the clarification of the problem.

Nicolai Hartmann's doctrine of the "stratification" *(Schichtenbau)* of the "real world" marks the transition from the traditional "unproblematic" attitude to a new comprehension of the world-concept. In its derivation from the epistemological problems discussed by the Neo-Kantians and in its attempt to overcome the limitations of their position, Hartmann's philosophic thought may be called representative of that turning-point of philosophy which, especially since World War I, was referred to as the "return to the object." Hartmann's conception of ontology—the core of his voluminous work—parallels one of the lines of evolution which proceeded from Husserl's "Logical Investigations." [52] Husserl had made a distinction between two strictly correlative queries inherent in every investigation of philosophic problems: the question concerning the modes of intentional behavior, on the one hand, and, correlatively, the question concerning the corresponding classes of objective facticities, on the other. The idea that each realm of entities is not only proportioned to a specific mode of experience but also possesses its own specific structure of being—that, consequently, entities are classified and distinguished according to regions, and that therefore the categories of each of these regions must be sought and identified—caused Husserl to start upon his project of elaborating these regional differentiations of entities in the form of corresponding *regional ontologies.*

This project was in very similar manner developed and systematically implemented by Hartmann who included in his synthesis the results of the individual sciences. More recent research has shown that this systematic synthesis is in part indebted to certain distinctions which are already formed in the work of the Neo-Kantians, Cohen and Natorp.[53] It is not possible to state definitely to what extent the speculation of Husserl, too, has left its impress. In the course of the elaboration of Hartmann's project it became manifest that the mutual relationship of the different regions and their categories was not one of simple juxtaposition but that these regions and their categories are vertically structured in layers and in part interpenetrate. In addition to the "fundamental categories" which determine each entity as such (harmony and conflict; identity and diversity; interiority and exteriority, form and matter), those other categories must be looked for which are the specific property of the four spheres or layers of all entities (the organic and inorganic, the psychical and the spiritual) or which permeate several layers. Thus each "layer of being" *(Seinsschicht)* has its specific categories. To the organic layer, for example, pertains finality, a property which is still lacking in the inorganic layer. Finality, however, is a category which has its place also in the higher layers or strata of the psychical and spiritual. The world is thus stratified not only in layers which are determined by specific categories, but the concrete particular entity, too, may participate in several layers and their categorical laws. Man, for example, partakes of all four layers. On the other hand, the fundamental categories change according to the way they appear in different layers. The fundamental category of determination, for example, manifests itself in the layer of the inorganic as causality, in the layer of the organic as finality, in the layer of psychical being as motivation, and in the layer of the spiritual as a "total context of meaning" *(Sinnzusammenhang).*

The turning away from the purely epistemological and scientific-theoretical approach of Neo-Kantianism, the phenomenological overcoming of psychologism in consequence of the new positive evaluation of the "ideality" of the logical and of spiritual "structures" *(Gebilde),* reached their greatest efficacy in this theory of stratification. As against the one-sidedness of many older philosophic doctrines—which either levelled the concept of being down to a "being-posited for a consciousness" or transferred a structural model borrowed from one of the strata of entities (for example, the model of a finalistically determined becoming or the model of atomistic mechanics) to the totality of that which is and in this way tried to interpret its composition—we meet here with the acknowledgment that predications about entities must comprise a variety of modes and that their constitution varies according to the "sphere" to which they belong. A way must be found to make manifest this diversity, a way which reveals the progressive disclosure of the world in the empirical sciences, and consequently the categories of the different strata can be determined only on the basis of the orientation which is provided by the individual sciences. The categories represent therefore the conceptual formulations deriving from the fundamental structures, structures which are disclosed in and give direction and guidance to experience. The ontological discovery of the categories of all entities is therefore a task which must remain essentially unfinished because it is progressing indefinitely. The status of this task at any given time contains the open possibility that by a future disclosure of new structures of entities in the course of scientific experience new categorial relations may be discovered.

Let us ask, however: what results from this doctrine of stratification with regard to *the notion of the world itself,* and in what respect has this notion already become a philosophic problem? It strikes us that nowhere in the writings of Hartmann is the notion of "the world" explicitly and thematically discussed. Only in passing, as it were, do we find the remark that what is at stake is the "real world," and "reality" is determined by temporality, that is, by that which is or exists within the one and all-encompassing time which comprises the entities of nature as well as the entity of man and the entities of history. Everything that "really" is has its place in the one time and receives therefrom its character as "reality," a character which differs from the being of that which exists ideally, i.e., from the supra-temporal nature of logical structures as well as from the forms of the "objective spirit."

The being of all that which "really"-is-in-the-world is interpreted with the aid of the concept of "inherence." Everything that really exists is inherent in the world as in the highest kind of totality. It has its place in this wholeness, and at this place it is "there" individually. But it is simultaneously universal, owing to the fact that it can be determined as this individual "being-there" *(Daseiende)* only by those properties of its essence (*Soseinsbeschaffenheiten*) which it shares with other entities. This particular pencil, for example, shares its being-brown with other brown objects. *This does not mean, however, that "existence" (Dasein) and "essence" (Sosein) are either opposed to or separated from each other.* "Such a separation exists only in thought, not in reality, where the essence of something is simultaneously also the existence of something (though not of the same thing), and the existence of something is simultaneously also the essence of something." [54] Through the concept of inherence, with the aid of which the being of that which really-is-in-the-world is explained, Hartmann thus attempts to annul the difference between existence and essence: "The essence of an existing entity denotes nothing else but *that* some definite determination 'is *there*' (i.e., exists) in something which is definitely determined." [55] If, therefore, one considers the total contextual reality of the world, within which every existent entity has its definite place according to its essence, the predications concerning existence *(Dasein)* and essence *(Sosein)* are convertible or mutually exchangeable: "certain characteristics of existence are manifest in the essence, and certain characteristics of the essence are embodied in existence." [56] For since the entire real world "exists only in the form of the singular," all the particular "places" which are occupied by a definite existent entity in its essentiality exist (i.e., are "there") only in the form of the singular and unique. This real total contexture *(Realzusammenhang)* of the world is thus "the true *principium individuationis.*" "Every essence (Sosein) as much as every existence *(Dasein)* acquires its determination on the basis of entire chains of determinations, and it is these latter which constitute the total contexture of reality. The isolated properties of individual things are abstractions. That which is 'really' real is also really possible and really necessary, even in its most minute features. But it is both really possible and really necessary because of complexes of conditions which encompass the entire breadth of a real collocation (*Realkollokation)* at any given time." [57] The *real total contexture of the world* is therefore, strictly speaking, not a *principium individuationis* but rather in its wholeness "individuation as such." "For it is because of ever novel real situations that processes and events always turn out differently." [58] Processes and events produce forever novel forms of existence at their unique position and in their unique configurations of essential determined properties. The "totality of the world" is thus not only the quintessence or the sum total of all that which really is, but this totality is that "whereon, wherein and whereby" all entities are, in so far as they are in the world. *In this totality of the world, existence and essence coincide,* inasmuch as its thus-ness *(ihr Sosein) is* determined by the amount of being which is "there" and which in its essence is determined by the world's total contexture.

This contexture of reality—in relation to whose totality, when seen in the perspective of its total determinateness, there is no difference between existence and essence—can, however, never be exhaustively grasped in experience but discloses itself step by step in its determinateness in the process and progress of scientific knowledge. It is thus the task and accomplishment of the individual sciences to disclose progressively the nature of the true world in the determinateness of its total contexture. Philosophy then conceptualizes by means of categorial analysis the structural contexture discovered by the sciences. The concept of truth that guides philosophy and philosophy's idea of science—directed toward the determined real contexture of the world—are in principle identical with the corresponding guidelines which prevail in the sciences. Philosophic categories are discovered in the same sense in which we speak of scientific discoveries, and their strata and interrelations which often at the moment of discovery are still veiled, emerge gradually. In giving this explication, Hartmann consistently refrains from denying that his system of categories, too, may well be partially invalidated by future research. His account of the history of philosophy therefore intends to trace the discovery and elaboration of the categories of existing entities in the past and to regard them as preliminary steps on the way to that clarification which is made possible by the present condition and status of science.

The preceding remarks may serve us to understand within what limits the investigation of the phenomenon "world" must of necessity proceed within the frame of Hartmann's ontology. He emphasizes that in the relationship of human cognition with its objects there can be no question of a production of the object by the agency of the subject because he sees cognition itself as an "ontological relationship" *(Seinsverhältnis),* that is, a relationship between entities of different strata. However, despite the fact that he therewith turns against neo-Kantian epistemology, Hartmann does not relinquish the ground on which this kind of epistemology has grown. This becomes evident (1) when Hartmann describes the task and function of philosophy as an indefinitely progressing process of the discovery of the categorial structures of the world; and (2) when he takes over from Descartes the division of the world into *res cogitans* and *res extensa.*[59] For "world" he understands quite self-evidently in the sense of an "external world" *(Aussenwelt),* as the world of reality in which all entities in their stratification and categorial order become accessible for the knowing subject, a subject which, to be sure, is not spatial himself but who—as a "real entity" *(real Seiendes)*—has, like all real entities, its locus within the stream of one and the same time. It is precisely this argument that provides the explanation for the fact that the possibility of the subject's cognition is described as an "ontological relationship." This relationship is subsequently explicated by Hartmann with the aid of the concept of "representation." The "forms of knowledge" (*Erkenntnisgebilde*) [60] are said to be "the counterparts of the objects to which the knowing spirit (mind) is ordained. Cognition is, as far as its contents are concerned, a realm of objective structures" *(Gebilde),* and this means, on the one hand, "real" structures, if they are acts of consciousness which, as psychological *facta,* manifest themselves in the stream of one and the same time and, on the other hand, "ideal" structures, that is, in relation to that which is cognized in them, as, for example, a doctrine or theory in its ideal unity. It is thus the nature of spirit to be "representation of the world, to be an image of the world within the world itself." [61]

We must ask here the question whether in this kind of thinking the "turning toward the object" which is represented in Hartmann's philosophy—that is, the turning away from epistemology—and which is supposed to lead to the restoration of metaphysics, is not accomplished by a *tour de force.* In other words, we must ask whether Hartmann, while overcoming the inadequate subject-object dichotomy, has not at the same time removed the genuine philosophic problem on which this dichotomy was founded. For he does not even pose the question as to what constitutes that distinguishing mark of the "spirit" which enables it to be a representation of the world. He fails to do justice to the peculiar "dual position" of the spirit, a position which enables it, on the one hand, to be a real entity (*real Seiendes*) in the world so that it becomes possible to say that cognition implies an ontological relationship, while on the other hand the spirit comprises the world in the mode of representation. Hartmann's categories offer no possibility of accounting for this dual position of the spirit. According to these categories, the being-in-the-world of every existing entity is determined by the concept of inherence: every entity is said to have its temporal abode in the one and only real world. It is true of course that those intellectual acts in which cognition is realized—pertaining, as they do, to the real existence of a human being—can be explicated by the concept of inherence. They are acts of specific somatic-psychical-spiritual being that has its definite locus in the total contexture of reality. But what makes them specifically spiritual acts is precisely their being-representation, their intentional relation to their objects, and this being-representation cannot again be interpreted with the aid of the concept of inherence.

Hartmann's conception of "being-in-the-world" (in the form of inherence) does thus not take account of the fundamental difference between "real" and "intentional" relationship. In other words, *the fact of "representation" pierces the structural stratification of existing entities.* True enough, the spirit—considered as a psychological datum—can be described as positing the intellectual acts of a knowing subject at a definite locus within the total contexture of reality as "resting upon" the lower strata of the somatic and the psychical. As soon, however, as the spirit's "representative" functioning, that is, its intentional relationship, is taken into consideration, it becomes evident that the image of a stratification is inadequate, because all the relationships of the strata to one another are "real" relationships among which there is no place for the unique quality of an intentional relationship. If the being-in-the-world is to be determined according to that which is "its exclusive essential property" (*eigenwesentlich*), the general concept of inherence proves inadequate. The temporal locus *(Zeitstelle)* of the spirit differs essentially from the temporal locus occupied by an inanimate thing or by a plant within the total contexture of the real world. It is thus the concept of representation which ruptures Hartmann's unified concept of existence, understood as a "standing in a real contexture of determinations." And the difficulties which are encountered in the attempt to interpret this concept on the basis of Hartmann's speculation make it evident that—despite the many subtle distinctions—the concept of being is levelled to such an extent that *the interconnection between "world" and "spirit" cannot come into view at all.* If this interconnection of an intentional relationship between the "spirit" and the "world" is taken seriously, it becomes clear that the "world" is not a firm, thoroughly determined, total contexture of reality into which the spirit—resting upon the lower strata of the somatic and the psychical—enters, as it were, only subsequently in order to disclose and illuminate this contexture step by step by means of scientific knowledge. It will rather become evident that the structural whole of reality and the meaning of its "stratification" cannot be understood without taking account of the intentional relationship that exists between the "spirit" and the "world." [62] Hartmann's fundamental insight that in view of the uniqueness of the world as an ultimate facticity the difference between essence and existence is annulled—that is, *his discovery of the facticity of the world's Dasein* (existence) first opens the way to making predications concerning the potentialities of its *Sosein* (essence)—cannot be understood in its real significance on the basis of Hartmann's premises. This insight in its true meaning points thus beyond itself to the task of comprehending the relationship of the "spirit" to the "world" as an intentional one.

It was this task which *Husserl* set out to accomplish. We shall therefore have to trace now—as the next step in the unfolding of the world-problem—Husserl's analysis of the world-concept. And we shall have to ask which problems remain still unsolved and therefore make it necessary to go one step beyond Husserl's answer.[63]

The goal which Husserl pursued in developing his method of *phenomenological reduction* was to find an adequate philosophic expression for pure and immediate experience. Accordingly, he was convinced that every entity must be queried in correlation to the operations of consciousness, on the basis of which the entity as such is present for us as a *datum.*[64] Now it is a fact that in our wakeful, conscious life we are as a rule intentionally oriented toward entities as objects of our perception, of our evaluation, as the aim and end of some volition or striving. This means that we are oriented toward particulars or toward universals, but not toward "the world" as a totality. Nonetheless, however, the world is not something that is entirely foreign to or something that transcends experience—as is the case with a transcendental idea—but the world is rather *a structure* which belongs inseparably to that which is experienced and according to the "how" of the experience. The world reveals itself as such as a structure in a dual sense and respect: first of all, it pertains to the meaning of each and every intentional content of consciousness that this content is self-evidently meant as an entity "in-the-world." The world is the universal "ground of faith" *(Glaubensboden)* upon which all judgments concerning any "being-thus" *(so)* or "not-being-thus" *(nicht so)* are performed.[65] No matter how much in the course of our experiencing our expectations may be deceived, our disappointment is confined to the judgment "this is not so, but different." Our disappointment never amounts to a total "naught" that would be totally destructive of our conscious life and render it meaningless. In considering the ways in which we can consciously and meaningfully posit something as "existing" *(seiend),* we begin to envisage the "world" as the universal "ground of faith" which is presupposed in all attributions of meaning. The world is thus *not one object of consciousness among others* but rather the broad stage upon which everything of which we can predicate "existence" *(es ist)* in any sense can make its appearance as something "given." The enunciation of this fact does not, however, derive from any subsequent reflection concerning the precondition of the possibility of positing something consciously in our intentionality as "existing" but rather articulates itself in the manner in which every existing entity as such is given in human consciousness. Addressing, for example, my perception to this desk, I grasp it as "my writing desk," "placed in this room," "in this house," and so on. To the meaning of positing an existing entity there pertains thus a background, all that which is co-intended and from which this particular thing stands out qua "*this*-thing-there." To every individual entity "given" to human consciousness there belong always certain references, pointing to further experiences as potentialities of experiencing: "I am able to go on from here, and if I do, I shall have further views and perspectives." It is not necessary that these references be always fully conscious, although they can always be actualized. According to Husserl, each and every individual given entity carries along with it its *horizon* of possible further experiences: first of all, its *spatial* horizon which, in its full concretion, constitutes our *Umwelt* (surrounding world), in which we live and which offers on all sides open possibilities of further experiences, so that this *Umwelt* is for our comprehension nothing else but that piece of "the" world which at this moment is accessible to us. The horizon is, however, also a *temporal* one: this desk, for example, stands there in my consciousness as the same desk which was already previously at the same place, the same desk at which I shall again be sitting to continue my work.

Thus it becomes manifest already in the analysis of the individual entity which is an object of an intentionally directed experience that every experience and whatever is experienced in it stands within a total horizon which we call "world." In other words, "world" denotes nothing but a fundamental structure of experience and, correlatively, of that which is being experienced. World is the horizon of all those actual and possible things which can be experienced, and this means that it is more than the quintessence of that which is and in which all individual entities inhere; and it is more than the sum total of ontological relations as such, as was Hartmann's claim. The relationship between "spirit" and "world"—which Hartmann accepts without any further questioning—is interpreted by Husserl as an intentional relationship, on the basis of his demonstration of the "horizon-structure" of all experience. The term "horizon" points already to the fact that *"world" cannot be understood as a neutral system of relations* but that it has a center. Horizon, after all, denotes literally the boundary of the visible, a boundary which continually shifts according to the standpoint of the seeing and perceiving subject. In this sense it may be said that everyone has, first of all, *his own world (Eigenwelt)* not only as the realm of that which is possible for him but as the quintessence of all that which constitutes for him the frame of his lived experience. In this sense we speak, in a phrase that is intelligible to everyone, of a person's more or less narrow or more or less wide horizon. His horizon is the sum total of what he already "knows," not only in the sense of theoretical knowledge but in the sense of his being thoroughly familiar with the ways of dealing with things in accordance with their already known properties, with their serviceableness, with their "value." The horizon is therefore always replete with possibilities. That which is already known and familiar points out the ways for future acting; it delineates the amplitude within which the aims and objectives, in particulars as well as in their totality, are permitted to unfold, including even the ultimate goals of life—the amplitude of everything that a person believes to be desirable and attainable. And the aims and ends of knowledge, too, are confined to that horizon. It is the horizon which determines the boundaries of what can possibly come into view as worthy of query and inquiry. And the result of such inquiry is the interpretation of some realm or region of being by means of scientific determination and explication.

The scientifically determined and explicated world, with respect to which we feel inclined to assume that it is—at least in progressive approximation—the world as such *(an sich seiende Welt),* can thus no longer be accepted as an ultimate, beyond which our questioning cannot extend. Since all scientific endeavor is a specific mode of intentional activity and since every activity with its particular objectives itself proceeds within limits set by a corresponding horizon, the inquiry into the nature of the world must be referred back from the interpretation which the world has received by scientific research, to the inquiry into what the world looks like prior to this scientific information. In short, the insight into the horizon-structure of the world makes mandatory a *retrogression to pre-scientific experience,* that is, to the "lived-world" *(Lebenswelt)* as it is experienced in its original immediacy.[66] Only in this way can the demand that a "natural concept of the world" must be gained—a demand already formulated by some representatives of Positivism (e.g., Avenarius)—be fulfilled. The phenomenological reduction as a method of restoring experience in its pristine purity does therefore not only amount to the demand that *each and every individual object* of experience must be subjected to an inquiry into the manner in which it is immediately given, the manner in which it is intentionally present in consciousness, but it also makes visible the "ground" *(Boden)* or the foundation upon which the experience of an individual object always rests in the process of its realization. And experience always does rest upon the foundation of a universal acceptance of the world by an act of implicit faith *(Weltglaube).* To get hold of this "ground" and of the world, as it is experienced in original immediacy, the presupposition of an objective "world as such" (*an sich seiend*)—this generally presupposed thesis of the natural attitude—must be set aside so as to make visible in what manner the total horizon is constituted in its structure by the realized experiences of the subject.

This retrogression to the world as it is experienced in original immediacy, as it is always co-present in the structures of whatever is experienced, must, however, not be misconstrued as if all the work of experience and the labors of science and their interpretations over a period of thousands of years were to be negated and as if it were proposed to revert to a dark pre-historic era or to the stages of primitive childhood because these primitive experiences are supposed to contain a higher truth. In view of this sometimes encountered and pardonable misunderstanding,[67] it becomes mandatory to point out that even the aporias which have resulted from certain queries of empirical science make clear the meaning of and the need for such a methodological "bracketing" *(Einklam-*

merung) of the "objective world." Under the rule of the tradition of "sensism" *(Sensualismus)* in psychology, for example, the notion of "sensation" *(Empfindung)* had been formed not by an adequate interpretation of the inner experience of sensation, but it had been rationally construed as a "sensed datum" *(Empfindungsdatum)* which was said to correspond to a quantitative stimulus that was objective-physically measurable. It was generally presupposed that a constant relationship must exist between the objectively measurable process and the sensation which was caused by it. What constitutes and causes a "stimulus" was thus not understood on the basis of the "sensed experience" but rather on the basis of the already physically interpreted world. The nature of the sensation, corresponding to the physically determinable "stimulus," was derived from a consideration of the laws which were prevalent in this physically interpreted world. The research of the gestalt-psychologists has proved conclusively that this theory of "constancy" is untenable because it is not supported by a real description of the psychical phenomena. The analysis of the tactile sensations has proved furthermore that these latter cannot be understood if the space staked out by the sense of touch is being equated with the homogeneous objective space of geometry. Similarly, the exploration of animal behavior in the animalic *Umwelt* has shown that the structure of the space ot the *Umwelt* cannot be assumed and presupposed to be the same—namely, a mathematically determinable space—for all living beings.[68] Again, in the field of psychopathology, the demonstration that phenomena such as anaesthesias or the phenomena of world-alienation, etc., must be understood as transformations of the individual's total world-horizon, points in the same direction. This transformation of the world-horizon imparts a change of meaning to all individual functions of sensation, of space-consciousness, etc. It is evident, therefore, that these functions cannot be referred back to an unchangeable ontological relationship between the recipient of stimuli and certain constant physically-objective "thingly quanta" *(Dinggrössen)*. And the analysis of the world of primitive tribes and their institutions, as it was undertaken by Gehlen,[69] has shown that the absolutization of a scientifically determinable objective world—resulting in the positing of an unreal "world as such," related to an unchangeable human nature, centered in a knowing rational subject—renders impossible the understanding and the reconstruction of the archaic world and its coherence as horizon of a meaningful and consistent behavior. Here, too, a more deeply grounded apriori of human nature and its world than that propounded in modern philosophy has been uncovered.

All these discoveries made by empirical science in its attempt to interpret phenomena adequately, testify to the justification of Husserl's radically different interpretation of the world-concept. From the already scientifically interpreted world as the sum total of all really existing entities *(real Seiendes)*—which as extended entities were supposed to have their locus in the one objective space—he turned back to that *Lebenswelt* which we really, immediately and truly experience.[70]

The phenomenological reduction is always a reduction to my very own "I am" and to whatever is consciously experienced within the I-am consciousness. Not only must the individual objects and their differences be explored as they are consciously experienced, but they must also be understood in their concrete individuality, that is, as consciously experienced within their particular horizon, a horizon which is always and immediately *mine*. Every human being has *his own* world, but in the process of the interpretation of what this "given" world contains of each individual's world, it becomes evident that according to its meaning the world is never *only* his own world. Every entity that enters my experience points in its meaning to those other human beings with whom I am "in-the-world." The desk, for example, at which I am sitting, carries (phenomenally) for me the meaning that it is a product of the work of a carpenter. In this sense then it may be said that everyone has *his own* world but what the world represents for him it does not owe to him alone. It has *become* for him what it *is* for him, but not only owing to those experiences which he himself has made in dealing directly with existing entities but also owing to the fact that he has learned from others how "one" behaves, how one makes value judgments, what one is supposed to know. That which appears to be self-evident to the individual derives from the way his fellow-men, especially those of his immediate environment, think concerning the world of things. In short, world as the horizon of that which is already known and familiar—the horizon which delimits and delineates the amplitude for all human behavior—is always already a *common or communal world.* All experience is, as it were, common-communal experience, but it is appropriated by the individual human being who, on the basis of such received participated experience, is now in a position to make novel experiences of his own. In applying everything that he has "learned," his own expectations are either fulfilled or frustrated. But what he has learned, too, does not remain exclusively his own possession: he communicates some of it to others and thus contributes to the enrichment of their experiences. We see thus that world—as horizon—is involved in a process of a continuous transformation to which everyone contributes his own share. The interpretation of the world by science, too, is nothing else but such a common experiential operation and achievement, a process in the course of which the common and universally valid elements can be distinguished more and more clearly from the "prejudices" which are held by individuals and groups. The scientifically determined world is thus the result of a common or communal orientation, and its interpretation—especially as far as the structures of nature are concerned—can be succesfully emulated and accomplished even by individuals who in all other respects, especially in their evaluations and therefore in their *Weltanschauung,* are separated from one another "by a world."

Does this not mean, however, that the scientific determination of the world signifies a liberation of man from the prison of his always limited horizons and perspectives, that the scientifically determined world is an approximation to the *true* world, the world that is in itself objectively determined? Is it conceivable that human beings, by means of their experiential performances could possibly create such a universally available system of orientation—named "scientifically determined world"—out of their own horizons and out of the aspirations conditioned by these horizons—if the total contexture of entities, as they are constitutionally determined in themselves, were not coming to their aid? The question therefore arises whether *the* world is not more than merely a system of orientation, formed and developed in the experiential operations and achievements of communities of men. Is the world not *more* than a structure consisting of socialized or communized subjects?

There is no doubt of course that it was the aim of Husserl's phenomenological analyses to comprehend the world as a structure *(Gebilde),* to demonstrate that the world owes its origin to the experiential operations and achievements of the community of subjects. Man's "being-in-the-world" therefore has for him a dual meaning: it signifies (1) that man lives already within his horizons, that he is an individual of this particular time and this particular community and therewith—as a human being "in this world"—within a definitely limited horizon. Man thus sees himself, as it were, from the outside, in the manner in which others see him, as the end result of all the processes of experiences which have led him to discover himself as this particular individual with this particular name, playing this particular role. Man's "being-in-the-world" means (2) that he is a center of intentional operations and performances and that he knows himself as a being who builds upon the foundations laid by others and thus transforms the already given world for himself and for others. Every new discovery, every new idea is such a transformation. And so it would seem as if Husserl's analysis of the world and its constitutive origin terminates once again in the traditional path of transcendental idealism. The difference lies in the fact that the central question concerns no longer the production of the object by virtue of the creative intellectual functions of the subject but—in a much more profound sense —*the central question concerns now the production of the world as the "wherein"* (das Worin) *of all possible objects, as* the horizon within which all individual entities stand out, so that they can be grasped and comprehended as objects.

To be sure, for the individual "world" is always "there" without his doing, without any action on his part; it is passively pre-constituted. But every passivity—as, for example, the passive acceptance of the knowledge that has been originally gained by someone else—points to some prior activity (perhaps the activity of a preceding generation), by which that which is now passively accepted, was originally acquired. It is the ultimate aim of Husserl's method of phenomenological reduction to understand subjectivity as activity in this latter sense. The phenomenological reduction is the means that makes it possible to understand the world in its totality as a structure that results from the free activity of the communized (*vergemeinschaftet*) subjects (that is, the activity of "inter-subjectivity"). "World" as the stage of everything that can be experienced, of all possible objects of consciousness, is then nothing else but a system of intentional poles of mutually communicating monads, the structure of their common mutual understanding and orientation. It remains thereby undisputed that the most perfect elaboration of such a "relational system" (*Bezugssystem*) of universal intelligibility represents the world view of objective science. However, the question as to the ultimate metaphysical interpretation of being as such (*das an sich Seiende*) is answered by Husserl in an idealistic sense.[71]

Nonetheless, Husserl's conception of the world as the horizon of that which is already familiar contains motifs which are conducive to a transcension of this idealistic conclusion (a conclusion which was also in line with Husserl's self-interpretation) and which tend to advance still further the understanding of the phenomenon "world." We can trace this advance, including the overcoming of Husserl's idealism, in the philosophy of *Martin Heidegger*. Although Heidegger's objections to Husserl's world-analysis are nowhere explicitly formulated, the direction which they take may be deduced from an interpretation of his own propositions.

In Husserl's philosophy man is continuously questioned as to how "world" is being formed in his experiential operations, as to how on this basis he is able to understand himself from the outside, as it were, as "man-in-the-world." In his very core man is a freely formative subjectivity; his absolute subjectivity is the starting point of all philosophic questions. The main theme of Husserl's thinking becomes therefore the formation of the world of objects and of his own self as an object named "man-in-the-world." All the structures which he builds refer him back to himself as the constitutive subjectivity which underlies these structures.[72] It is thereby presupposed that the ultimate reason or "ground" of the constructive formation of "world" is to be found in the free activity of man's subjectivity. However, it is precisely this presupposition that must be called in question, because it implies an inadequate interpretation of the subject's "being-subject" (*Subjektsein*).[73] Husserl obviously does not recognize that free formative activity, the constitutive production of a world, cannot exhaustively describe the depth of the nature or essence of the "subject," since what really and most deeply concerns the subject is his "being-in-the-world," and the subject must already have experienced his "being-in-the-world" as problematic and threatened before his formative activity can begin to function. The query must therefore be extended *beyond the formative activity of the subject* to the predicament and distress in which the subject is immersed and which provide the stimulus for his building the house of the world around himself. This means then that "world" cannot be understood as the product of intentional operations: it cannot be understood as that "wherein" man in his *Dasein* always finds himself.[74] The "in-being" in the world does thus not denote (as it does with Husserl) that man, as this particular objectively determinable individual, comprehends himself as one object in the world among others, related to them ontologically; nor is it sufficient to say that man "is always embedded within some horizon." For to have an horizon means to feel already at home in the world, to live already within a circle of known and familiar entities which determine every step of human life. That human life formatively creates this circle constitutes the human *response* to the fact that life in these familiar surroundings feels itself constantly threatened. Man's response seeks safety and security in view of a threat which must have pre-existed and which induces him to actualize and deploy his multiple activities.

The answer to the question as to what constitutes this threat will reveal the basic features of Heidegger's analysis of "world" and will show to what extent it leads us beyond Husserl's investigations.

What threatens man is, according to Heidegger, not any definite events which may happen in the world, any dangers the imminence of which man may fear and about whose aversion he may be able to reflect. For if man is said to be threatened by some definite entities, it is presupposed that he is a being who is capable of placing before his mind's eye (*vorstellen*) the possibilities of what may happen to him as well as the possibilities of how to behave in view of what is going to happen—a being, in other words, capable of conceiving a *project* of his future. We must ask then: what is it that is projected in this project? What is projected is the definite manner or mode in which man exists at any given time, the manner in which—in view of what he anticipates and fears—he is nonetheless capable of coming to terms with and of making himself feel at home in his world. What is at stake in all that is feared and anticipated is man's very existence. He knows that the manner of his behavior in view of that which is imminent, the answer to the question whether he will be able to cope with the objects of his fear or whether he will fail, depends on him. In his behavioral reaction to the challenge he decides about the "how" of his existence. The possibility of fearing something definite, of feeling himself threatened by something definite is thus rooted or "grounded" in his *freedom* of making a decision in one way or another, either failing and foundering or authentically proving himself. This does not mean, however, that Heidegger attributes to man a *liberum arbitrium indifferentiae:* he does not mean to assert that it is impossible to inquire into the motivations of human behavior. He rather regards human freedom as that *fundamental structure of human nature* (*Wesen*) which makes it possible to understand man as a being who acts in accordance with certain motivations, as a being who is basically and essentially capable of letting his actions be determined by *deliberation.* In the process of deliberation the possibilities of action become more or less articulate. Man understands himself in his possibilities, and he acts on the basis of this understanding. Freedom thus denotes nothing else but this always "being-ahead-of-oneself" in projecting the possibilities of what one can be and how one can act accordingly. The structure of freedom is therefore the a priori presupposition for an understanding of man as a willing and acting being as well as for any moral judgments concerning his actions.

Man's existence is thus basically a "being-outside-himself" (*Aussersich-sein*). The nature of man cannot be defined as a sum total (*Inbegriff*) of qualities and properties, on the basis of which his behavior could be calculated as a composite structured according to the rules of a natural law, as a result of his descent, his "potentialities" (*Anlagen*), his acquired habitudes and the experiences embodied in them. When these factors, which determine human actions by virtue of motivations, are understood by means of deliberation, they are no longer blindly operating forces. When, for example, man adapts himself to some constraining necessity, this is already a *self*-adaptation and no longer a blind reaction. This "being-ahead-of-himself," this "being-outside-himself"—which makes us understand how man is possible as precisely this particular individual self, taking hold of himself in self-experience—Heidegger calls the *transcendence of Dasein*. But whither does *Dasein* transcend? The answer is: *to the world*.[75] To transcend does therefore not mean that the subject in his apperception "steps outside himself" (*heraustritt*) to move toward the objects, nor does it mean the apperception of this or that particular object: transcendence rather denotes that fundamental structure which constitutes the essence of human freedom. Transcendence makes it possible that man is "in" the world at all and that he *has* a world. For to *have* a world does not simply mean to stand over against something that is definitively given; it does mean a continuous behavioral "stepping beyond" the given by making the given the stage upon which man's personal potentialities are brought into play. To have a world is understood by Heidegger as something which delineates for personal *Dasein* the possibilities of its being, possibilities which as such must be seized by *Dasein*. In this seizure *Dasein* understands itself not as finished but as a being-possible that is guided by the project of what it can potentially be. In the service of this project stands the mustering observation (*das Durchgehen*) of that which is given, with the result that the given stands out as an object and can be seized in knowledge. Transcending is thus a "stepping-beyond" the totality of that which is (*das Überschreiten des Seienden im ganzen*). This does not mean a "stepping-forth" from the *Ego-cogito* to reach particular individual entities; it does mean a "stepping-over" (*Überstieg*) toward that "wherein" all existing entities as such are first encountered—a "stepping-over" toward the world. Transcendence is thus the *world-project* of *Dasein*.[76]

This does not mean, however, that "world" is nothing but a "formal structure" (*Gebilde*) produced by *Dasein*, as if *Dasein* as such were world-less and would project a world by means of its constitutive activity. *Dasein*, as a matter of fact, can project itself upon its world only as the sum total of its potentialities—its "horizon"—because it exists itself already "in the midst of existing entities" and permeated by them: *Dasein* itself is already "worldly." It can therefore not be primarily conceived as a thinking subject that produces the reality of objects by the syntheses of thought; it can exist as a thinking subject, appropriating his world through the activity of his thinking, only owing to the fact that it already finds itself placed amidst existing entities. Its potentialities are therefore not free and unlimited *ad libitum* (*beliebig*), since it is always and at all times deprived of a certain number of possibilities. What is it that accounts for this deprivation? The fact that it is actually always this or that particular *Dasein*. In its project it does not choose its world freely, since the world-project is a "thrown project" (*geworfener Entwurf*). This means that *Dasein* must be understood as essentially *finite*. And finitude means to exist actually already in a worldly manner but to project itself comprehendingly in this act of existing. The sum total of all these structures is the *facticity of Dasein*.[77] *Dasein* is free, but since its freedom is a "thrown" freedom, it is not absolutely free (*seiner Freiheit nicht mächtig*). This limitation of *Dasein's* freedom reveals itself in the modes in which it encounters itself, above all in the mode or state-of-mind (*Befindlichkeit*) of "dread" (*Angst*). In dread the threat to *Dasein* and the nature of that which threatens it become most clearly manifest. *Dasein is threatened by its own facticity*, by its potentiality of a freedom which yet is limited and relative. The anxious dread, therefore, relates to the threat to its freedom and thus to that which is the very core of *Dasein*.

Now we are in a position to ask: what progress beyond the content of Husserl's analyses has here been achieved with respect to the problem of the world? Husserl's analyses had already shown that "world" cannot be understood as an isolated system of interrelated existing entities but must be conceived as having its center in a "zeropoint" (*Nullpunkt*). This center, however, was not seen by Husserl in its full concretion. The factual world in which human *Dasein* finds itself at any given time is conceived by him as a constitutive structure, related to an absolute starting point that marks the basis on which the inquiry into the essential possibilities and the different types of world-formation rests. What is bypassed here is the facticity status of this point of relational reference, a point which cannot again be re-presented (*vergegenwärtigt*) to serve as a directive for an analysis of essences. "The actuality (*das Dass*) of the facticity cannot be encountered in an act of perception."[78] This means that the facticity cannot be envisaged from the standpoint of a theoretical observer who is situated in a supra-historical absolute starting point of philosophic inquiry; it can be encountered only if the inquirer enters into the historical situation within which the questions are being asked. Every philosophic problematic has to submit to this law if it claims to be a genuine inquiry rather than an arbitrary inquest. The latter is condemned to sterility from the outset, regardless of whether this arbitrariness and sterility are realized in philosophic reflection or whether they remain obscure on account of the opinion that an absolute supra-historical starting point has been gained. Husserl's point of departure, too, is therefore really not absolute. The retrogression to the Cartesian I-am and the ensuing necessity to find a way back from the isolated ego to the world, which are the determinants of Husserl's method, reveal themselves in this perspective as the necessary consequences of the historical fate which rules over modern thought and determines its limits. But to perceive and understand these limits accurately means that they have already been transcended.

It becomes thus evident that the question as to the nature of the world as that which is always "there," cannot be answered by a realistic "turning toward the object," a movement which simply accepts existing entities in their manifoldness without inquiring into their categorial structures. From this point of view man is conceived of as merely one entity among others, an existent who in his relationships with other existents of the same species resembles all other entities. Against this point of view the justification of demonstrating the creative and formative operations of subjectivity by means of a constitutive analysis must be maintained, because only in this way does it become possible to understand the scientifically interpreted world in its categorial structure as resulting from the human "will to know" (*Erkenntniswille*). The *idealistic interpretation of the relational interconnection of "world" and "human subject" is thereby invalidated,* since the interpretation of the nature or essence of the world makes it mandatory to push the inquiry into the nature or essence of man farther than would be possible by means of an analysis which has to rely exclusively on finished structures. It then becomes manifest that "mood" or "state-of-mind" (*Befindlichkeit*) pertains to the fundamental structure of human existence—a structure which in Husserl's analysis of passivity is indeed referred to but which is not recognized in its full significance, chiefly because Husserl—within the frame of his idealistic self-interpretation—tried to reduce all passivity ultimately to the active operations of subjectivity. But the passivity implied in the "finding-oneself (already and always)-in-the-world" cannot itself be again dissolved in the formative operations of absolute subjectivity. What manifests itself in this passivity is rather the facticity of the "being-in-the-world," *a facticity which can never be abrogated.* It is evident therefore that we can never—in the manner of philosophic realism—inquire into the nature of man as if he were simply one entity among others, receiving "stimuli" from these others, considered as his objects. That from which the stimuli emanate is here conceived of as subsisting in itself in the sense of objective scientific determination. Nor can we resolve this problem of man as an "object-in-the-world," entertaining ontological relations with other objects, into an inquiry concerning the activity of an absolute subjectivity that formatively underlies all these ontological relations—a subjectivity which experiences itself in the freedom of its reflection as the ultimate ground of these formative processes. This would mean that what is already and always "there" as "world" would be idealistically annulled, and the origin of all being would then be situated in subjectivity. To avoid this fallacy, we must ask first what it is that makes it possible to "receive stimuli" and what it is that makes it possible to exist as a being that has sensory perceptions and sensations. The answer is that it is the "world" as a thrown project which makes all this possible—the world in whose structure of "mood" or "state-of-mind" the possibility of stimulus-reception and of sensibility in general is grounded. In other words, sensation and sensory perception—those ancient themes of psychology—cannot be understood as states of an isolated subject that erects his world upon a substructure of sensory atoms or sensory forms (*Gestalten*) through the medium of the synthetic operation of intellectual judgments. Sensation must rather be understood as a structure of "being-in-the-world." As such it is sensed auto-motion, a movement in which the spatiality of the world discloses itself. Seen from this point of view, the psychological concepts of sensory datum and sensory *gestalt* reveal themselves as products of a methodological attraction rather than as concepts of the ultimate structural elements of consciousness.[79]

A clarification of the world-concept in Heidegger's sense may thus also serve to provide a foundation for a philosophic interpretation of the insights contained in the most recent trends in psychology as well as in the explorations of the *Umwelt* in the field of psychopathology. Far from being a mere philosophic construct, Heidegger's world-concept is a valid interpretation of that consciousness of "world" that does not only harmonize with that immediate understanding of "world" which becomes articulate in everyday matter-of-fact predications concerning the world but also with the results of empirical research. Although the latter had already shaken the construct of the positivistic world-interpretation, it had not been able to appreciate fully the philosophic significance of its own findings.

CHAPTER III

The World as Nature

While up to this point we have been speaking of the general basic determinations of the concept "world," we shall now have to show in what direction the philosophic interpretation of the world is being carried on in several particular fields. We will not concern ourselves primarily with a discussion of philosophic theories but rather with the consideration of those specific philosophic problems which derive from the present status of the natural sciences and from the question concerning the extent to which the previously presented views of the world-concept are conducive to a resolution of the aporias to which recent research in the natural sciences has led. This does not mean that philosophic knowledge should be measured by the results of the knowledge gained in particular sciences as if only the latter could provide a criterion of philosophic truth. The concept of philosophic knowledge is always too narrow when it is understood exclusively as "scientific theory" *(Wissenschaftstheorie).* The question as to the fruitfulness of a philosophic clarification of the world-concept with respect to the interpretation of the knowledge gained in the individual sciences will help us to recognize that both philosophic thinking and scientific research are characterized by a common basic attitude regarding existing entities.

It is of course well known that the development of natural

science has for a considerable length of time proceeded in almost complete separation from the development of philosophic thought. The reasons are of a historical nature, and a consideration of these reasons will reveal the peculiar character of the present-day interrelation between philosophy and natural science.

Ever since the beginning of modern times the foundation laid by Descartes accounted for the conviction that one and the same epistemological method was valid and applicable in philosophy and in the natural sciences. Kant was the last one among the great modern thinkers who developed his system on the basic premises of natural-scientific thinking. It is only in the last decades that we have learned to see again that Kant's critique aimed at a reconstruction of metaphysics rather than at merely laying a firm foundation of natural science.[80] In the service of this task, that is, the reconstruction of metaphysics, Kant limited the realm of rational knowledge—which since Descartes had submitted to the absolute criterion of "clarity" and "distinctness"—to the world of "phenomena." He thereby established a definite boundary for the natural sciences: they do not disclose an "in-itself" (*ein An-sich*) of substance but only the contexture of phenomena. He held firm, however, the basic conviction of modern times that scientific knowledge signifies the intellectual domination of all existing entities ("phenomena") and thus the predictability of the contexture of phenomena as it reveals itself under definitely established conditions. To this extent at least it remains for Kant an unquestioned fact that human knowledge signifies a seizure of power over all existing entities—that is, over the world of phenomena—on the basis of an insight into their lawful contexture, as interpreted a priori in the categories. Kant's philosophy was thus the last philosophic system that was capable of providing guidance and direction to natural science, a guidance which has proved efficacious even to this day.

However, even in Kant's own lifetime, the antagonism between him and Herder indicated that from then on philosophy was no longer able to maintain the supposed absoluteness of the concept of reason (*Vernunftbegriff*) upon which modern philosophy from Descartes to Kant had been built. The relationship of man to reality, founded on the concept of reason—a relationship which was also regarded as the foundation of the natural sciences—was, owing to the evolution of historical thinking,[81] itself understood as an historically conditioned and delimited mode of the understanding of "the world" and of "the self." Ever since Hegel philosophy was forced to look for its foundation in an encounter with history and with the historical disciplines, and as a consequence the interconnection between philosophy and the natural sciences was more and more lost sight of. Even today the natural sciences are looking in vain for a philosophy which might be able to provide the needed guidance in an attempt to lay their own foundation. Even in those instances where they actually did engage in philosophic reflection, their recourse to philosophic systems of the past or present has remained more or less arbitrary and unsatisfactory because of these systems' inability to do justice to the genuine impulses of scientific inquiry. It was first necessary for the natural sciences to bring about—forced by their own specific problems—a complete reversal of their own presuppositions, before they could dare to hint cautiously at the meaning of this revolutionary event and its relation to the radically changed outlook in philosophy.

The foundation of "classical" natural science—that is, of the kind of natural science exclusively dominant from the beginnings of modern times to the early twentieth century—was the presupposition that the "objective world," the universe of all existing entities, was a world completely self-contained and determined in itself—regardless of whether this world was conceived of in the terms of metaphysical realism as "being-in-itself" or in the Kantian sense as the idea of the totality of phenomena.[82] All scientific knowledge was referred to this self-contained objective world, a world in which the knowing subject is opposed to the sum total of objects. This idealization of that which is "determined-in-itself"—which was simultaneously formulated in the principles of logic [83]—implied the conviction that it is the function of all knowledge to unveil an already existing truth. This meant to say that all the interconnections among existing entities are strictly determined in and by themselves, and that it is only owing to irremediable imperfection of our human knowledge—which can never comprehend the totality of the conditions underlying an event—that an event may appear to us as merely probable or merely fortuitous. A divine Reason of the type of Laplace's World Spirit would therefore be capable of deriving from the perfect knowledge of some specific world-condition the totality of the events which of necessity precede and which of necessity follow from this condition. *This conviction of the total determinateness of all existing entities* is the actual foundation of classical physics and thus the foundation of modern natural science. It is easily seen that the latter rests upon the strict separation of the knowing subject from the "external world" of objects, a separation which ever since Descartes has divided the totality of existing entities into the two realms of the "internal,"—the immanence of consciousness—and the "external," the spatially extended. This latter in its lawful order was regarded as strictly mechanically determined.

From the very outset the phenomenon of "life," which can neither be understood as consciousness nor simply as extended mechanically moved matter, posed great difficulties. The inadequacy of the machine-theory of organic life was felt already in the eighteenth century, and attempts were made to resolve this difficulty by having recourse to the theory of pre-formation. According to this theory, it must be assumed that for every character determination of the fully grown organism a particular determining "life"-factor must be present in the nucleus of the fertilized egg. This means that in the fertilized egg cell all those structures "whose fully developed form is the finished organism" must already be "pre-formed." The germ cell is thus supposed to be an infinitesimally image of the fully grown organism, and the development of the latter would then be merely a kind of "unfolding" (*Auswickelung*). This theory is thus an attempt to explain the process of the evolution of life as taking place within the frame of the causal pre-determination of everything that comes to pass. The wholeness of the organism is thus assumed to be the summary result of the formation of the actual individual parts, on the basis of certain pre-given individual structures which can be physico-chemically verified.

The inadequacy of this theory was demonstrated convincingly by *Hans Driesch,* and his conclusions were definitely substantiated by the attempts made by *Spemann* and his school to transplant living germ-fragments.[84] These experiments showed that the finished form is never pre-determined in any living germ cell or in any of its living parts. The preconditions for the formation of an organism are not predesigned in its physical structure. Each of the two halves of the egg of a sea-urchin can, after their division, develop into a—correspondingly small—organic whole. And transplanted parts of an organ can, according to the site to which they have been transplanted, take over entirely different functions. It is this capacity of "self-differentiation" (Spemann) which has no analogon in the realm of the inorganic that cannot be accounted for within the frame of the classical physical world-view and therefore gave rise to various attempts at explication. It was Driesch's conclusion that some specific "integrative" (*ganzmachend*) factor must be at work in the organism, a factor which eludes the grasp of physics. Inasmuch as the realm of the physical is understood to be a realm of extended materiality, this factor cannot be spatial in its nature; it can be no quantitative extension; it must be some supra-material agent. To name this agent, Driesch reintroduced the term *entelechy*. Accordingly, he states that it is the function of the "entelechy" to create order in some physical, spatially extended quantity of matter. In his later writings, however, Driesch reverses his theory when he states that the image of some order-creating agent within a given quantity of matter is inadequate, since the specific function of the organism consists in acquiring for itself the material upon which order is to be imposed.

It may be said then that in the construction of the living organism two factors cooperate: the entelechy and the forces which determine physical matter. But this schema is still too simple; for the condition of chemical substances within the living organism cannot be identified with the condition in which these substances are found outside this living union.[85] The former condition is characterized by a special kind of unstable equilibrium that is again and again restored in the processes of metabolism, assimilation, and dissimilation. A chemical analysis of these processes cannot cast light on the way in which this unstable equilibrium is being maintained. In short, the metabolic process is not the foundation of life nor does it constitute the essence of life; it is rather an effect or sequel of life. If we then apply Driesch's theory to this state of affairs, it appears that it is the function of the entelechy to control and steer these processes. If this control ceases, there ensue multiple chaotic chemical reactions, and the organism perishes. It would seem then that the life processes are indeed chemico-physically determinable, but they do not owe their origin to purely chemical processes. This means, however, that—despite the thoroughgoing chemico-physical determinability of the occurrences within the organism—the processes in the living organism and those in dead physical matter differ essentially.

Driesch subsequently attempted to define even more precisely the point at which the ordering and integrative efficacy of the entelechy takes a hand. In doing this, Driesch took full account of the development of modern physics. This efficacy extends beyond atoms and molecules, reaching out into the intra-atomic structure, into elementary particles, into electrons and protons. The view that the steering processes in the organism which determine the functions of individual parts are of micro-physical subtlety has been confirmed from other sources.

In the theory of *vitalism* as formulated by Driesch we must distinguish between that which is based on irrefutable experimentally secured findings and that which itself is but another theory that serves to explain these findings. Irrefutable are the facts of *self-organization* and *self-differentiation*—facts which exclude any pre-determination and which make it mandatory to look for the factors by which this self-organization is directed. Irrefutable is also the statement that the vital impulses of this direction are to be sought in the realms of the micro-physical. Mere theory, on the other hand, is the re-introduction of the "entelechy" as a factor that accounts for the non-spatial, ordering, and integrative functioning. It is this theoretical aspect of Driesch's discoveries which is denied recognition in present day biology. With the term "entelechy" Driesch introduced a concept which in reality merely expresses the embarrassment which is caused by the abortive attempt to explain life mechanistically. This concept explains actually nothing, nor does it point to any methodological possibilities with respect to the exploration of organic life. Such an exploration is conceivable only on the basis of a comparative study of an organic and an inorganic system and their structural laws. It is therefore the most important feature in present day biology that, without paying heed to any theories, it looks for these differences in structural laws and thus arrives at a critical rejection of the claim of vitalism to have furnished a principle of explanation of organic life by the introduction of the concept of the entelechy. *Woltereck,*[86] for example, points out that the dynamism of vital processes can be accounted for by the excitation of non-spatial interiority, an internal spontaneity which is not a mere urge but an intentionality directed at a definite aim, an intentionality which is subject to guiding ideas, that is, to the leading impulses or the determining determinants of all becoming. These latter, however, must not—contrary to Driesch's opinion—

be understood as timeless values that are superimposed on the contexture of becoming but as forces which are exclusively at work within the living units themselves.

Without any such definite reference to the nature of an ultimate active principle that is supposed to underlie the life processes, *Bertalanffy* and *Dotterweich* [87] have developed *a theory of the dynamic equilibrium,* according to which the difference between a merely chemical system of balance and that of a living organism is to be found in the fact that the latter presents us with an *open system.* "Any closed system, according to the second law of thermodynamics, must pass over into a non-temporal state with maximal entropy and a minimum of active energy. The chemically balanced state is incapable of any operation. The performance of work requires that the system be not in the state of equilibrium but rather strives to attain equilibrium. Therefore a steady feeding with material quantities and energies is needed in order to keep the system constantly in a certain distance from total equilibrium and thus capable of operation." [88] This schema makes it possible to represent all the characteristic phenomena of life, such as metabolism, growth, structural formation, excitability, as consequences of a "fluid equilibrium" *(Fliessgleichgewicht)* and to grasp the specific nature of life by contrasting it with those chemico-physical processes which take place in the realm of the inanimate, without, however, attempting any interpretation or predication with respect to that which keeps this "fluid equilibrium" in motion, that is, without construing a "metaphysics" of life which might feel tempted to substitute a mere word (such as "entelechy") for the chemico-physically inexpressible and intangible "ground" of life.

The concept "fluid equilibrium" serves also to clarify another important matter: the preservation of the organic system in stationary repose. In contrast to the crystal, for example—whose self-identity rests upon the identity of the structurization of its own matter—the living cell persists in its identity despite a continuous change of the matter. *Plessner* [89] calls this capacity the positional character of life: life posits itself in whatever it is, by reaching out beyond itself by means of assimilation and metabolism. While the inanimate body exists only to the extent of its spatial reach, the organic body always transcends itself and its spatial boundaries. While it is true that the organic body is self-enclosed and while the cell closes in upon itself in the process of cell-division, it nonetheless enters into a relation with its neighboring cell by means of osmosis. The realm of organic life is such a system of continuous self-limitation and is as such embedded in a related surrounding "field" *(Umfeld)* from which it draws its nourishment and into which it releases certain material substances *(Stoffe).*

This relatedness of the living organism to a surrounding "field" has been studied by *Jakob von Uexküll* with special reference to the higher stages of the animal organism.[90] He developed the so-called *Umweltforschung* (i.e., the exploration of the animal's surrounding world), which is based on the principle that a living being can be understood in its particular individuality only by investigating its relationship to its *Umwelt* which always has its own specific spatiality and its specific qualities of content. It is, according to Uexküll, the very nature of a living being *(Dasein)* to create for itself such an *Umwelt.* This *Umwelt* is a unity of meaningful active energies which are attuned to the structural design of the living being. Every organic system is thus strictly adapted to its specific *Umwelt,* and there exists a direct relationship between the *Umwelt,* the vital activities *(Lebensäusserung),* and the structural designs of the animal. Uexküll's investigations were carried on by *K. Lorenz* with an inquiry into the schemata which, in the form of so-called "instincts," determine the behavior of animals and which are inherently present in every animal genus.[91] The exploration of these *Umwelt* schemata and their corresponding schemata of behavior has become of decisive significance for the understanding of animal behavior. The investigation, for example, of what a living being endowed with sight actually sees, has shown that what becomes at all relevant as a stimulus in the animal's *Umwelt,* is—

within an identical environment—entirely different according to the specific structural design of the particular living being. As far as we ourselves are concerned, things differ according to the optically perceptible form which in many instances points to their suitability for our personal use, as is the case, for example, when we perceive some tool. In the case of lower living organisms, on the other hand, the form does not act as a stimulus at all. It is different with the bees: representing a higher stage of organization, they react to certain simple formal differences which are relevant in their life-cycle to identify honey-bearing blossoms. It is thus evident that what constitutes "sensation" for a living being cannot be determined on the basis of the objective-physical nature of the objects. The results of these investigations, too, demonstrate *the untenability of the concept of sensation held by sensist psychology* and by Positivism, and they testify conclusively to the need for Husserl's method of "bracketing" any presupposition of an "objective-world-in-itself." [92]

We must remain acutely conscious of these results of empirical biological research because they signalize a significant change in our view of nature. Let us ask then: what is the philosophic meaning of this change?

Whereas for classical natural science nature was the sum total of the spatio-temporally extended and of that which is objectively determinable and subsists in-itself, *vitalism* started out from the assertion that in this system of nature—considered as a system of strict pre-determination—life with its specific phenomena could find no place. But Hans Driesch still maintained that the quantities of matter which entered into the entelechy-directed organic wholes must be spatially localizable and spatially determined matter.[93] The theory of a dynamic equilibrium, Plessner's interpretation of the life-phenomena by means of the concept of positionality, and Uexküll's *Umwelt* research have demonstrated on their part that there is a correlation or correspondence between the highly developed living organism and its surrounding "field" and have thus shattered the presupposition that life can be comprehended as a process that, though determined by non-spatial factors, must nevertheless—as far as physico-chemical aspects are concerned—be essentially enacted within an absolute space and within the one absolute time. *These concepts of an objective space and an objective time cannot be maintained.* But even if space, in Husserl's sense, is interpreted as a structure of the world-horizon and is referred back to the constitutive operations of the subject, such an interpretation cannot be squared with the facts that have been disclosed by biology and *Umwelt* research. For though not every living organism exists in the mode and manner of a subject, it is nonetheless more than mere extended matter that moves in a space which is objectively one. Every living organism has rather its own specific space-schema, in accordance with its organization. This space-schema is neither that of the objective mathematical space, nor can it be deduced from the synthetic functions of the consciousness of the human subject.

All theories, moreover, which seek to attribute the origin of organic movement to some non-spatial interiority which is supposed to steer the external events, are products of the embarrassment that is caused by the fact that one has failed to dissociate oneself from the idea of the one objective space in which all sensorially perceived events are supposed to be localized. These theories result once again from different kinds of interpretation; they are not based on scientific findings. However, they relinquish the inescapable *question as to the real nature of that physico-chemically determinable matter which enters into the organic processes* and is then subordinated to the latters' specific lawful order or pressed, as it were, into their service. Classical physics believed that it was the objectively and spatially determined atoms as such whose movement was conceived of as manifesting itself in the form of processes in objective space. Owing to the fact that contemporary physics in the most recent phase of its development has shaken this conviction, it is making its weighty contribution to fashioning a new relationship of man to nature, a relationship which brings in its wake new possibilities of interpreting the meaning of the life processes. In the following brief appraisal of the significance of this development it will be seen that it leads to a juncture which philosophic reflection has reached by different routes independently, a point of juncture which is also the aim of the biological exploration of life and its functions.

The first shattering of the seemingly self-evident presupposition of classical physics that all processes were determined in and by themselves in the one objective space and the one objective time—a supposition which was supported by the assumption of an absolutely static ether—derived from the difficulties posed by the generally accepted ether-physics. These unresolved difficulties led Einstein within the context of his theory of relativity to the insight that metric statements concerning spatial extension as well as temporal duration and temporal relations never denote absolute determinations which pertain to objects and events as such *(an sich)* but are meaningful only if they are referred to some specific system of relations *(Bezugssystem)*. The idea of an absolute simultaneousness of two events was herewith abandoned. The two events are simultaneous for one observer, while for another observer, who is in a different state of motion, they are "successive." *Minkowski* concluded from this premise that the three dimensions of space must be united with the one dimension of time to form a mathematical relational system of four dimensions. Space and time function here only as axes of coordinates in a four dimensional system. "In such a system one can no longer speak of events. The only real event is here the successively experienced perception on the part of a subject moving alongside the continuum." [94] The theory of relativity leaves still room for an interpretation of the contexture of the world as a thoroughly determined system, since time can here be interpreted as the necessary form in which the phenomenon of the self-contained and once and for all established universe appears to human reason. The demonstration of the impossibility of this theory was furnished by Planck's discovery of the "quantum of efficacious energy" *(Wirkungs-*

quantum), that is, by his insight that the laws of radiation and light can be described accurately only when the radiation is not understood as a continuous process but as a process which progresses, as it were, "by leaps" in smallest quanta. The further exploration of the laws of light-radiation has found its provisional conclusion in the discovery of the dual nature of light—as wave and as corpuscle—which was formulated by Heisenberg in his "uncertainty principle" (*Unbestimmtheitsrelation*).

In what respects then does quantum mechanics differ from classical physics and what are the philosophic implications and consequences of quantum mechanics? "It has discovered that one and the same physical object has two different forms of appearance which seemingly exclude each other: the particles and the field (or wave). These two forms in which all atomic objects manifest themselves in scientific experiments are not selected from a large number of equivalent possibilities: they rather are characterized by a complete disjunction. A particle is a physical structure which when it is found at one place cannot simultaneously be at another distant place. A field, on the other hand, is a structure which permeates space. The particle-nature of a structure can be deduced from all the experiments which demonstrate a localization of its effects (as, for example, in cloud chamber photographs). The field-nature of a structure in turn can be deduced from all the experiments which prove a combined working efficacy of several locations separated by some distance *(Interferenz).* What, then, can be the meaning of the statement that an electron is both a particle and a field? Experience, to be sure, shows that electrons produce both kinds of effects (localization and *Interferenz*). But can this seeming contradiction be resolved? As a matter of fact, there is no contradiction, as far as the actually observed properties of the electron are concerned; the contradiction appears only when one assumes that these properties are properties of the electrons even if one refrains from observing them." [95] This statement, however, implies more than merely saying that the different answer which nature gives to the question concerning its structure depends in each instance on the kind of question that is asked in the experiment, as if it could be assumed that some substratum *(ein Zugrundeliegendes)* that is thoroughly determined in and by itself manifests itself now in one way and now in another. If this were the case, the experiment would serve no other purpose but to create the conditions for this manifestation. But this is not so. That which manifests itself—whether it be wave or corpuscle—is rather *produced* by the experiment, in accordance with the nature and arrangement of the experiment. "It depends on our freely chosen experimental arrangement which of the mutually 'complementary' aspects of nature we perceive, and the knowledge of these conditions *(Sachverhalt)* excludes the knowledge of the complementary conditions." [96] It is therefore meaningless to ask: what is the appearing phenomenon "in-itself?" "Quantum mechanics differs from classical physics in that the former cannot even pronounce its propositions without co-pronouncing the particular kind of knowledge that is involved." [97]

It becomes therefore mandatory to relinquish the *Cartesian separation of subject and object* and to abandon the attempt to regard the "objective" as if it were "being-in-itself," of which definite predications can be made, predications in particular relating to specific quantities determined-in-themselves. "The quantity which in quantum mechanics determines a state of the atomic object—the φ-function—indicates the probability of the results of certain experiments. The term 'state' *(Zustand)* relates to the acts of observation. We cannot speak here of an object in separation from a subject." [98]

We are now prepared to refer cursorily to the philosophic consequences which follow from these insights. *It is no longer possible to speak of the being of nature without relating it to the being of man*—man understood not as an *abstractum* but *man in the concretion of his corporeality*. The relationship between man's corporeal quantity as a somatic being and the quantity of the object which he observes is by no means irrelevant with respect to what the experiment discloses as the being of nature.[99] On the basis of this quantitative relationship the instruments to be used by the observer—instruments manipulated by the observer—are of macro-physical dimension. The penetration, therefore, into the realm wherein matter forms itself, represents an intrusion which not merely affects that which manifests and discloses itself but even takes a hand in its production and construction. The problem of the compatibility of human freedom and the rigid determination of the realm of nature becomes thus groundless. This problem rested upon an absolutization of nature, whereby nature was regarded as a self-contained and in-itself-determined contexture—a concept whose fallacious nature has been proven by modern physics. This does not mean of course that the principle of a thorough-going causality must be denied. This kind of causality is rather presupposed, and without this presupposition it would not even be possible to establish the conditions for the carrying out of scientific experiments. What *is* denied is a thoroughgoing determination of the contexture of nature, *independent of the being of man.* This does not mean that to the elementary particles can be attributed a kind of freedom of choice and decision analogous to human freedom. It does mean that from the fact that the ϑ-function indicates only a probability of the results of possible experiments we derive an *indication of the nexus which exists between the contexture of the being of the physically disclosed nature and the being of the freely acting human being, who intrudes into and interferes with the contexture of nature by subjecting it to his experiments.* The ultimate structural elements of matter can accordingly not be understood as extended quantities determined in and by themselves in an objective space. We are rather forced to the conclusion that *the specific character of the spatiality of those quantities*—either observable changes in the location of a corpuscle or wavelike expansion in some "field"—*owes its specific constitution to its relationship to an observer.* In other words, the elementary particles must first enter into the world of the observer before they can acquire a spatial determinability at all.[100]

These insights have important consequences with respect to *the problems posed by the phenomenon of "life."* We are no longer permitted to ask: "In what manner do non-spatial factors—such as entelechies or organizing agents—intervene in spatial physical processes?" For it does not make any sense to use the methods of physical research to explain certain facts which elude the grasp of physical science. This fallacious approach rested on the assumption that physical processes are spatially "determined-in-themselves." But since the steering centers of organisms are of micro-physical size, and since in the realm of the elementary particles—where the cause of their effects is located— the objective spatial determinateness does not exist, *the inquiry into the relationship between physical processes and organic growth must be placed on a new foundation.* "A concept of life which must make room for itself by artificially splitting what is physically interconnected, appears to me as a mere stop-gap in a dual sense. It is offered as a substitute for a God who himself is only recognizable by the yawning gaps or breaches of a world which he himself has created." [101] Just as quantum physics has not abrogated classical physics but has only confined it to a more limited realm of validity, so today's physicists are of the opinion "that physics must now be expanded in order to enable it to understand life." They are convinced "that there are specific laws of life and that the lawfulness of inanimate matter represents an outer limit *(Grenzfall)* in the same sense in which classical physics was an extreme outer limit of the quantum theory." [102]

The objection raised against the idea of a possible unity of physics and biology—that a living organism cannot be produced experimentally and must therefore be subject to conditions different from those which prevail in the physical inquiry into nature—is invalid. This inability to produce a living organism might suggest the idea that nature, too, has its unrepeatable history, in the course of which one unique constellation was necessary to generate life. Once the objectivistic assumption of natural processes that are determined in and by themselves in an objective space has been abandoned and the necessary connection between the spatial determination of matter and human observation has been established, the next step—suggested by the idea of the relativity of natural processes—will be *to understand the contexture of nature itself as a historical and non-reversible fact.*

If the question as to the being of "nature-in-itself"—a kind of being which recedes farther and farther from the experiments of the physicists—is to have any meaning at all, the answer cannot possibly be given by natural science itself. For it was natural science, after all, which in the course of its own development arrived at an insight into the inescapable relativity of the being of nature, only to be subsequently led to an acknowledgment of the signal importance of the observing human being for the disclosure of the being of nature. The nature disclosed by natural science does not *possess* a being that is subsequently recognized by man; it rather *receives* this being by entering into the historical world of man and by being subjected to the experiments conducted by man. Only to the extent that nature can be subject to this kind of operative manipulation, can it said to be "nature" in the sense of being the object of natural science, and only on this basis can natural science become an efficient tool for the technological domination of the world. None of the determinations which natural science receives from nature can therefore be exempt from this relativity with regard to the concrete somatic being of man. This does not mean, however, that nature is nothing else but a constitutive structure of subjectivity in Husserl's sense. Husserl's stipulation, on the other hand, *that the "in-itself" of nature* can be discovered only by a regress to pre-scientific experience and to the pre-scientifically apprehended and comprehended world-structure, remains valid. However, the being of nature which is implicitly contained in this pre-scientific experience, cannot in turn be reduced to the formative activity of the subject [103] but must be understood as that structural element of human *Dasein* that indissolubly belongs to the world and that adequately describes the mode in which

Dasein "is placed in the midst of existing entities" *(Befindlichkeit inmitten des Seienden).* We have already observed that "world" has a center: it is related to the felt and sensed movements of man, movements by means of which the spatiality of his world is being disclosed.[104]

What is revealed first of all in such an interpretation of nature is its character as *the earth* which both sustains and opposes man. This is what Husserl had in mind when he demanded a "reversal of the Copernican revolution." [105] In his last philosophic investigations Husserl devoted extended considerations to the phenomenon of the earth, regarded as a fundamental structural element of the world-horizon. These considerations came too late to effect a change in his basically idealistic position. It is only in Heidegger's philosophy—even though at first only in some intimations—that *the interconnection of earth, truth, and the concealedness of Being* becomes manifest.[106]

Let us try to understand Heidegger's thinking in this matter. To experience nature in its truth—a truth which cannot be established in the manner required by the "scientific method"—means to experience nature as "earth." This in turn makes it necessary to understand man with a view to what relates him to the earth, that is, with a view to the fact that he is a somatic-sensory and sensitive being. The earth and matter as entities which nourish and sustain man in his life can both be firmly grasped and dominated by man. However, this grasp becomes more and more elusive in the very process of trying to get a firm grip, so that eventually this increasing elusiveness leads to the insight that earth and matter must not be understood as space-filling objective substances, determined-in-themselves. This insight in turn points to the fact that what sustains and shelters man—that which exists "in-itself" in the sense that it is neither posited nor dominated by man—is simultaneously something that withdraws itself from his grip. *The truth of the Being of nature is therefore to be found not only in nature's overtness for scientific knowledge but simultaneously in this self-enclosed and concealed withdrawal movement*. It is, however, the structure of this withdrawal movement which "grounds" human *Dasein* as such in its historical facticity. This *Dasein* can constitute and re-constitute itself again and again, but only at the moment when it relies on the overtness and the concealment of that Being which determines the fleeting moments in the history of man.[107]

But if it is true that the lesson which we can learn from the development of natural science tells us that nature can be disclosed only by entering into the historical world of man, and that all scientific determinations are related to this historical world, then we shall have to inquire now into the "historicity" of the world.

CHAPTER IV

The World as History

The clarification of the world-concept in contemporary philosophy which has aided present day thinking in surmounting the abstract opposition of "world" and "ego," of object and subject, and in making intelligible "the world" as a structure of human *Dasein,* makes possible also a new interpretation of the nature of history. History can no longer be simply understood as events which are enacted among human beings on the firmly established stage of a world of objects which exist in-and-by-themselves, as if a changeable world of history were structurally superimposed upon a static world of nature. For if "world" is actually a structure of human *Dasein,* then the possibility of the pre-scientific and scientific interpretation of the world as nature as well as world-interpretation in a pre-scientific or scientific understanding of the historical past will derive from this structure. History must thus be more than a mere sequence of events effectuated by human action, events which eventually terminate, as it were, in a specifically pre-determined present. The mode and manner of appropriating the historical past knowingly and comprehendingly rest rather on the "historicity" of the deepest layer of the structure of human *Dasein,* a structure which constitutes what we have called *Dasein's* facticity.[108] In other words, *historicity is a fundamental structure of Dasein as "being-in-the-world" and therefore of "world" itself.*

To elucidate this concept of historicity and to investigate its connection with the fundamental structures of the world, is one of the basic problems with which contemporary philosophic thinking is preoccupied. However, the problem becomes articulate only gradually, in the process of the repudiation of opposite tendencies. In the following pages it will be our task to trace the several stages of this development in present day philosophy.

Hand in hand with this development goes *a new conception of the nature and the objectives of the philosophy of history,* and from the central significance which attaches to "historicity" within the total contexture of the structures of human *Dasein* derives the insight that the philosophic inquiry into the nature of history ceases to be merely one special problem among others but presents itself as a fundamental problem which determines the structure of philosophy as a whole.

According to a still widely held opinion, the philosophy of history is a *speculation* on the course of world history as it has been explored by the science of history, in the form of *subsequent reflection.* This reflection—in separation from the course of history—seeks to answer the question whether there is any "meaning" to be found in the course of historical events, either in the sense of a progress toward a definable goal or, conversely, in the sense of a process of decline, or in the sense of a cyclical movement of the return of identical formal structures *(Gestalten).* This question thus asks in the final analysis whether a general law can be observed or established in these historical movements. This kind of philosophy of history is—with some justification—rejected by most historians as a barren construct which does violence to the course of historical events and which cannot furnish any guiding principles for concrete historical research. Even a cursory survey of contemporary works dealing with the problem of history shows that questions of this kind play a very insignificant role because a new style of questioning has become prevalent.

The ancient question as to the "meaning" of history has in many instances been equated with the question of whether there is any "progress" in history. The result was that with the waning of the belief in progress—a process which has been going on for more than half a century—it seemed to become more and more difficult to see any "meaning" in history. In the inquiry into the "meaning" of historical events two basic possibilities were discussed again and again: was there a cyclical movement in which eternal "forms" were realized, or was there a linear movement toward a definite goal by which "progress" could be measured? While the former question derives from the thinking of antiquity, the latter question derives from Christian thought. It was only with Christian revelation—regarded as an event that enters into history and can be temporally localized in it—that the idea of a *direction* of the course of history toward a final goal became possible.[109] For Christianity this goal was located in the lifeto come (*im Jenseits*), and the modern belief in progress has resulted from a secularization of this Christian idea. Man was no longer regarded as being embedded in a transcendent process—a process that extended from the Fall of man to the Last Judgment—but the forces of reason that are active in man himself, and the basic moral law of man's free will which with the aid of reason is capable of mastering the passions—that is, the forces of the *lumen naturale*—were said to propel human history toward a final goal. Progress was thus understood as *the progress of reason* and of the rational formulation of the world, as the self-realization of an autonomous human reason which unaided by divine grace and revelation was regarded as capable of obtaining those necessary norms and standards upon which right action and the supremacy of the human spirit over the earth could be founded.

It was *Wilhelm Dilthey* who in his historical research commented on the meaning and traced the origin of the idea of progress.[110] But it is above all in the Anglo-Saxon world that this idea has to this day retained its force and has thereby determined the philosophic inquiry into the nature of history.

In contemporary German thought, on the other hand, the idea of progress has experienced a crisis—a crisis which was by no means altogether provoked by the experiences of two World Wars but which has much deeper roots. In Germany the waning of the belief in progress has led to that novel kind of historical inquiry which characterizes contemporary German thought in general. In the rest of the Western world the incentives to the fashioning of a new relationship to history came—for the reason already cited—not so much from the philosophers than from the historians. But, as far as the results are concerned, a similarity with the basic tendencies of German thought is undeniable.

The new attitude toward history was being prepared by the evolution of the "historical consciousness" which occurred as early as the end of the eighteenth century. Wilhelm Dilthey was once again the first one who understood the significance of this development as a vital force which determined the totality of modern life and human behavior about the turn of the century. He was the first one to devote extensive historical research to an inquiry into the origins of the historical consciousness. This research was then in Dilthey's own school of thought carried on by such thinkers as Erich Rothacker.[111] A different aspect of the same development was presented on a broad foundation in Friedrich Meinecke's *Entstehung des Historismus* ("The Origins of Historicism," 1935). When Meinecke speaks of "historicism," he has in mind the historical consciousness as such rather than its decline into skeptical relativism, a connotation that is usually connected with the term "historicism." He tries to understand historicism in general as a specific phase in the evolution of the Western mind, as "the highest stage in the understanding of things human hitherto attained."

What then is the characteristic feature of the historical consciousness and in what respects does it differ from that historical attitude which finds its most distinctive expression in the idea of progress? If the course of history is regarded as a progression toward the actualization of the potentialities of human reason and its supremacy, then all those epochs of history which precede the attainment of the final goal, are reduced to mere means to be used on the road that leads to the attainment of the final goal. *Herder* had already opposed this idea: "Not one single thing in God's total Kingdom is a mere means; everything is simultaneously means and end." Herder thus is of the opinion that the overemphasis on the idea of progress leads of necessity to an underestimation of the individual character of different historical phenomena and epochs. It is, after all, the goal of the modern historical disciplines to articulate the historical structures and events in their individual and unique significance, in contradistinction to the attitude of natural science which regards such structures and events as typical actualizations of universal laws. Historical consciousness means therefore an understanding of history as the development of individual structures: its basic characteristics are *the ideas of evolution and of individuality* (Meinecke). And Leopold von Ranke's demand "to tell what has really happened" *(sagen, wie es eigentlich gewesen ist)* is likewise oriented toward this kind of understanding, an understanding which does not attempt to "mediate" the individual epochs by reducing theme to mere means, but tries to understand them individually in their own particular nature. They bear their standard of measurement in themselves and can therefore not be measured by supra-temporal norms.

If, however, this basic demand—not to measure historical phenomena by a supra-temporal standard but always to derive the standard of our measurement and our understanding from those phenomena themselves,—has any validity, then such an attitude must extend also to our own period. But here the question arises immediately whether in this case certain obligatory norms for human action can be found at all and whether the consciousness of the relativity of the standard of measurement of every historical phenomenon must not also apply to our present age. The consequence of such an admission would be that no universally binding norms for human action can any longer be found and that there remains nothing but a surveying understanding of the course of history, without any criteria for the right or wrong in our own actions. For, if the presupposed relativity of the standards of measurement is a fact, then all the goals of human striving are relative with respect to the standards of value of any particular time, and they are subject to change with the changing times. It was these seemingly skeptical consequences deriving from the historical consciousness which has preoccupied contemporary thinking as "the problem of historicism," especially following the first World War. Although the problem as such has never been philosophically resolved, it has today largely disappeared from our consciousness. It has merged, as it were, with the more general problem of the nihilistic devaluation of all the norms which guide human existence. We shall have more to say on this subject in Chapter VI, where we will deal with the problem of "knowledge and action."

Toward the end of the nineteenth century the problem of historical relativism appeared at first to be of a purely scientific-theoretical nature—an inquiry into the meaning of the knowledge acquired in the historical disciplines, including both the science of history in the more restricted sense and the humanities or "human studies" *(Geisteswissenschaften)* in general. The problem was formulated by the "South-West German School" of *Wilhelm Windelband* and *Heinrich Rickert* as an inquiry into the meaning and significance of a knowledge which does not—as does scientific knowledge—understand the individual as a "case" of applied universal laws, but wants and claims to be a knowledge of the individual and the singular. The problem was posed in this school as a query concerning those principles of selection, according to which that which is of significance for historical knowledge is being chosen. Here, too, the presupposition of an amorphous reality of "the given," which only by virtue of the operations of reason presents the picture of a meaningful contexture, was taken for granted. The principal question was this: "How do individual events of the past become history?" How do they become scientifically disclosed and comprehended history? And by what norms can the truth of the historical knowledge of individual events be measured and judged? [112]

Dilthey, too—following the general trend of the age—understood in his early period his inquiry into the meaning of historical knowledge primarily as a scientific-theoretical question and accordingly regarded it as his task to furnish a "critique of historical reason." [113] As Kant—at least according to the interpretation of the Neo-Kantians—had attempted in his "Critique of Pure Reason" to lay the foundation for and to justify the methodology of the natural sciences, so Dilthey regarded it as his task to develop a methodological foundation for the "cultural sciences." But this undertaking led him immediately to a series of much deeper problems, problems which centered in the insight that the "cultural sciences" were (as all the other scientific disciplines) themselves products of "life" which had their origin in the innate tendency of life to move toward ever higher levels of reflective consciousness. The inquiry into the foundations of the "cultural sciences" thus turned into an inquiry into *the structures of human life and its historicity,* from which, like all the scientific disciplines, all the "formations" *(Gebilde)* of life proceed as "objectivations of the spirit." Life "objectifies" itself; it "expresses" itself in its formations, and this expression—its objectivation—is always relative with respect to the corresponding stage of vital reflection which as such is subject to the respective historical conditions. Every historical epoch is founded on a basic constitutive set of conditions—Dilthey speaks of "vital moods" or "states-of-mind" *(Lebensstimmungen)*—which determine the character or the "spirit" of an epoch in everything it produces. All historical formations —and this includes the changing kinds of scientific encounter with the "given"—must be understood on the basis of these underlying "states-of-mind." However, in view of this relativity of every historical phenomenon, historical reflection becomes conscious of the "continuity of that creative power" which is nothing but the "unfathomable power" of life itself, which is sustained by this striving for ever higher levels of reflection and objectivation.

The principle on which Dilthey's argument rests is that of a *"purely immanent" interpretation of human-historical life.* Life must be understood "from its own innate nature and tendencies" (*aus ihm selbst*) without any reference to "metaphysical" interpretations. The latter, he argues, derive from a supposed efficacy of transcendent powers, whether they be conceived of as Divine Providence or as Absolute Spirit. The structures of life are interpreted with the aid of the "categories of life," whereby "life" is not understood in the biological sense but as self-conscious life, as that which in its structures is directly accessible "from within." In this way the structures of life become accessible in "psychological" analysis, an analysis which, as "understanding psychology" differs essentially from a merely "explicative psychology." The former can neither be a mere psychology of inner experiences (*Erlebnispsychologie*) nor can it be an experimental psychology which concerns itself with individual acts and behavioral attitudes in their psychological context and their psychophysical pre-conditions. The full concreteness of the contexture of inner experiences as it becomes accessible "from within" in reflection, can be grasped only in the objectivations in which these inner experiences express themselves. Psychological reflections and the historical contemplation of these objectivations have to rely on one another. The objectivations must be traced back to the inwardness which finds its expression in them, and this inwardness becomes intelligible only by viewing the ways and manners of expression, in using "a method which proceeds by the way of expression." The necessary "circle of understanding" is grounded in this mutual relationship.

With this new perspective Dilthey initiated a turning point in the understanding of history within the realm of German philosophic thinking. This had become possible because he was the first one who tried to comprehend philosophically in the fullest sense the significance of philosophy's encounter and dialogue with history, a dialogue which can be traced from its early stages in Herder to its full elaboration in Leopold von Ranke. Dilthey himself understood the significance of his own work in this way: "I wanted to communicate to others the life-mood which has grown out of my reflections on the consequences of the historical consciousness." [114] While in Ranke, who was Dilthey's teacher, the "historical school" reached its perfection, Dilthey had regarded it as his specific task to comprehend philosophically what had already happened in Ranke's—that is, the practicing historian's—encounter with history. For Ranke "stops short of the analysis of and the conceptual reflection upon the composite contexts which are co-efficacious in history. This marks the limitations of his historiography." [115]

It is a not yet very widely understood consequence of Dilthey's new methodological approach that *the separation of the historical from the systematic approach to philosophy is thereby revoked.* For, if Dilthey's insights are taken seriously, every systematic investigation must be conscious of the historical horizon in which it is embedded and of the perspectives—deriving from tradition—by which its validity is limited. On the other hand, every historical investigation of past modes of life that aims at the discovery of their objectivation in forms of society, of religion, of science, of art, and of philosophic systems, must explicitly take account of the limits which are set for any fully adequate understanding of the past by the situation of the present and by the specific horizons of its understanding. This reciprocal relationship in its entire revolutionary significance for the traditional structure of philosophy did not fully enter Dilthey's conscious awareness and, as a consequence, the vital connection that exists between Dilthey's historical and systematic-philosophic investigations remained hidden for a considerable length of time. But without an awareness of this interconnection the prevalent contemporary manner of understanding the historicity of human *Dasein* remains inconceivable.

Dilthey's suggestions were accepted and continued in different directions, although their ultimate foundations were at first not made the object of a basic philosophic reflection. His insight that all historical objectivations are sustained by a "life-mood"—by a "ground" upon which the totality of all the behaviorial attitudes of an epoch rests, a ground which impresses upon all its products and creations a homogeneous style—has led to the attempt to trace the manifestation of this fundamental relationship in definite "types." *"The Types of Weltanschauung"*—a work of Dilthey's old age—initiated a sequence of comparative studies of "types" of human behavior and of stylistic forms.[116] However, every such attempt at creating a "typology" runs the risk of surrendering again the fundamentally new perspective of history which had become possible through Dilthey's earlier research. For any typological comparative study—especially when it aims at finding in history the return of identical types—presupposes that it is possible that a *standpoint outside history* can be gained, a standpoint from which the types actualized in history can be contemplated as if they were a series of Platonic ideas. The question which preoccupied Dilthey from the outset—that is, the question to what extent this kind of a contemplation of the fundamental structure of life and its ligation to the intelligible horizons of a particular "present" is possible at all—is here in danger of being completely forgotten.

In a different direction, this striving for a "typology of *Weltanschauungen*" (different philosophies of life) and styles led to the attempt to lay a foundation of the "cultural sciences" (*Geisteswissenschaften*)—especially of "literary criticism" (*Literaturwissenschaft*) in the form of *a general* "history of mind and spirit" *(Geistesgeschichte)*. The concept of *Geistesgeschichte* and the demand to place the interpretation of individual works of art and literature within the total contexture of the evolution of mind and spirit, had in all essential features been prepared by the work of Dilthey. The concept of "mind" or "spirit" had been divested of that metaphysical connotation and component (that can be traced back to the influence of Hegel) and had come to denote the "ground" of that homogenous character which impresses upon the works of every epoch their specifically determined style. This perspective of *Geistesgeschichte* included also the philosophic systems, and it was this extension to the field of philosophy which eventually revealed the limitations and the weaknesses of this kind of approach. For the attempt to inquire into the roots of the evolution of mind and spirit—the roots of all the productions and creations of *Geist*—and to distinguish these roots from the merely external manifestations, had been abandoned. Since within the frame of reference of *Geistesgeschichte* the philosophic systems are regarded as mere "expressions of life" *(Lebensäusserungen)* on the same level as all the other "objectivations" of an epoch—as indicative of the manner of their self-interpretation—the question as to their philosophic truth is silenced. From here it is only one step to that "theory of ideologies" which derives from a further theoretical development of Marxism, a theory which sees the radical ground of all objectivations in the "real" economic factors of historical life and admits objectivations in Dilthey's sense only in the form of "superstructures."

The weakness of the further elaboration of Dilthey's suggestions regarding typologies of the most diverse kinds lies in the fact that in these developments those investigations of Dilthey which relate to *the systematic structural analysis* of the dynamic nature of human-social *Dasein* and their manifestations in the "categories of life" are being neglected. For there is no doubt that only such a structural analysis can lead to those insights which make it possible to make predications as to the propulsive forces of history and as to the meaning of the concept of "spirit," if "spirit" is to be regarded as a genuine fundamental category which as such can serve as a guiding principle for the laying of a foundation of all historical research and all the typological distinctions and differentiations within the frame of a "history of mind and spirit" *(Geistesgeschichte). Erich Rothacker's* investigations in particular are preoccupied with these problems. Aside from his aforementioned research in the field of the history of the "cultural sciences" and of the historical consciousness in general they are concerned with an inquiry into the roots of all the actually applied methods of *Geistesgeschichte*—roots which in most instances are not clearly discernible but which determine the scientific practice to a large extent as unquestioned presupposed convictions. But these typological distinctions with respect to basic philosophic attitudes, on the basis of which Rothacker in his "cultural anthropology" tries to understand individual civilizations and their culture as "styles of life" (*Lebensstile*), are not regarded as that which is ultimately "given" but are (in his "philosophy of history") traced back to the fundamental structure of human *Dasein*.[117] He starts out from the dictum that man must be determined in his nature as an "acting being." All action, however, means "acting-in-a-situation," whereby "situation" denotes the "inwardly experienced horizon" *(Erlebnishorizont)* or the manner and mode in which he has understood his own self, the manner in which he knows about himself. His situation conditions those "intuitive ideas" *(Einfälle)* which make it possible for him to master his situation as well as the specific tasks which derive from this situation. In short, human action is the response to the human situation. In addition, even these naturally given component factors which pertain to every historical situation are not to be understood as causal factors but rather as structural elements of the situation in which man attains to self-understanding and to which he responds in his behavior. These factors, inasmuch as they are comprehended by man, serve as motivations for his actions. The human condition is thus, on the one hand, "pre-given" *(Vorgegebenheit),* while, on the other hand, it is modified by human action. It is therefore the task of a structural analysis of human-social *Dasein* to trace this reciprocal nexus in all its relations and contexts, in order to show how, on the one hand, the historically acting individuals are already embedded in the medium of communal life—Dilthey had already attempted to comprehend the individual as a crossing-point and a turning-point of historical forces in the efficacious context of history—and how, on the other hand, those same forces transform the form *(Gestalt)* of the community and impart a definite direction to its innate tendencies by their efficacy. The alternative as to "whether it is men who make history" or whether history is the result of supra-personal forces, is thus shown to be inapplicable to the understanding of the dynamics of history because—like any "philosophy of the subject" *(Subjektphilosophie)*—it starts out from an isolation of the individual subjects and thus overlooks the fact that man is what he is only in the manner in which he has himself already been formed by a community while he, in turn, impresses his formative stamp on the community. In this reciprocal dynamic relationship those habits are being formed which determine the behavior of the individual and of society: what comes thus into being may be called the "style" of a community or an epoch. In this sense then civilizations and cultures may be comprehended as "styles of life" which impress a definite behavioral "attitude of life" (*Lebenshaltung*) upon each and every individual. In this sense it becomes meaningful to speak of "the world" of an age or a society, and this meaning is tangible enough to be described and analyzed. Rothacker's research has thus succeeded in circumscribing *the task of a comprehensive investigation of the correlation of world and man,* a correlation which must be presupposed for any human action.

Gehlen examines the question of "cultural styles" from a different angle by tracing it back to pre-historical times.[118] This is the first time since the publication of Ernst Cassirer's "Philosophy of Symbolic Forms" (*Philosophie der symbolischen Formen,* 1923 sqq.) that the problem of "primitive cultures" became again the theme of a philosophic treatise. Gehlen starts out from the findings of his anthropology,[119] which is based on the conception of man as an acting being. The institutions of archaic life and the categories by means of which they are to be understood and interpreted constitute the main theme of his discussion. They are characterized as the "externally crystallized manifestations" *(der Aussen-*

halt) of the habitudes by which the behavior of the primitives is guided and to which it owes its stability and homogeneous style (p. 24 sqq.). The forms of the ritual and the early ritually conditioned modes of artistic formation exercise a representative function in a dual sense: they produce the communal self-consciousness, and they stabilize the original experience of nature as a sympathetic coordination of man and world (pp. 167 and 200). Of methodological interest in this approach is the conviction that *Dasein* and the style of behavior of the primitives, too, can be recognized only by an analysis of the expressive manifestations. Dilthey's concept of the "objective spirit" appears to Gehlen too narrow to describe these manifestations adequately.

Even the earliest tools are, according to Gehlen, "petrified concepts." And he asserts that only by following his own method and nomenclature can the archaic cultures become accessible in their internal rationality as well as in their total strangeness. This strangeness is so heterogeneous that it cannot be understood if by "understanding" we mean not mere empathy but rather a "re-living" *(Mitvollzug)* of the impulses for practical behavior that are inherent in the primitive world-view (p. 133). For between those cultures and our own are interposed the thresholds of two distinct cultures: (1) that of monotheism with its concept of world-transcendence (whereas the archaic cultures do not transcend "beyond" the world but "into" the world); and (2) the world-view of the age of technology (p. 110). But here, too, we find that this kind of knowledge need not necessarily lead to the skeptical, relativistic consequences of "historicism," but may serve to broaden the much too narrow modern conception of man and to reveal the "inviolable normative rules" (p. 287) to which human nature is unconditionally bound to conform.

All these new approaches show a common methodological characteristic in that they are equally applicable to a number of separate disciplines. What has been accomplished by the analyses of Dilthey, Rothacker, and Gehlen on the higher levels of human-historical *Dasein,* was initiated in the realm of animal life by the *Umwelt* investigations of Uexküll and others. And it is only this analytical method which can provide the answer as to the basic ultimate forces which underlie and determine the course of history. The insight into the structures of human-social *Dasein* forbids us to assume an anonymous dialectical process as the essential motivating force of historical evolution, whether it be a process of the self-unfolding of the Absolute Spirit or—in the Marxist reversal of this Hegelian schema—a process of material conditions, conditions of material-economic production. For the conditions of production, too, are the result of human cooperation. As "given" conditions they are structured elements of a situation, a situation which in its turn is being changed by human cooperative action.

That contemporary thought—even when it derives from different premises and presuppositions—follows a similar course, is documented—to refer to only one outstanding example—by the great historical work of *Arnold Toynbee*.[120] Like Dilthey, Toynbee starts out from the contention that the traditional, metaphysically grounded, comprehensive interpretations of history, which tried to give an answer to the question concerning a single definable meaning of the goal of world history as a whole, are untenable. For Toynbee an organological interpretation of history, as it was attempted by *Oswald Spengler* and *Kurt Breysig*—which tries to understand the origin, growth, and decline of world-civilizations as cycles of organically growing forms—is equally unrealistic. There remains then only the way of a *descriptive analysis* which must start out from the actuality of a definite number of diverse and particular civilizations rather than from a postulated unity of the history of mankind, a postulate which was meaningful only within the frame of reference of the Christian world-view. The historian must therefore find the criteria for marking off different civilizations from one another, and he must ascertain how many civilizations [121] have been actualized in the course of history. These latter must then be descriptively compared as to the conditions of their growth and their common characteristics. The significance of Toynbee's work lies in this descriptive comparative analysis which deals with an abundance of hitherto practically unknown subject matter, while Toynbee's answer to the question concerning the philosophic presuppositions and consequences of this kind of analysis is—from a methodological point of view—insufficiently developed. What Toynbee has in common with other representatives of contemporary thought is the turning from speculation concerning the "meaning" of history to a descriptive analysis of the factors that are at work in history.

The significance of this development lies in the fact that the inquiry into history is freed from the too narrow frame of a mere scientific theory—a mere epistemology of the "cultural sciences"—and that the scientific dialogue of man with his history and its products is being related to the analysis of human *Dasein.* This methodological approach makes visible man's "historicity" *as a fundamental structure of his "being-in-the-world."* This structure shows most lucidly that "world" is not the sum total of objectively given entities existing in and by themselves but rather the situational locus in which man finds himself embedded at any given time. This "wherein" *(das Worin)* of man can, seen from one aspect, be interpreted as nature and, seen from another aspect, as history. The latter interpretation implies man's "always-finding-himself-in-a-situation" which man comprehends as his very own. He always finds himself situated in his "ground" *(Boden),* but in such a manner that this "finding-himself-embedded" is illumined by a certain amount of understanding. The situation—that which compels him to act, that which represents for him a task to be mastered—is not a sum total of objectively given entities but the manner in which he already knows himself embedded in the midst of "given entities," and it is on this basis that he understands himself in the possibilities of his actions. This self-understanding delineates for him what he is capable of comprehending as a possible goal of his actions; for any kind of action is possible only on the basis of a representation of definite aims or ends. Action is thus not a free projecting of possibilities but is conditioned and therefore limited by tradition, that is, by the remote origins of the individual and historical human situation. What man is at any given time therefore depends on the manner of his already actualized self-understanding in the world and within the frame of the possibilities of his behavior. His actual and factual existence thus constitutes his nature or essence in his historical situation. This nature or essence in turn is not a sum total of supra-temporal possibilities, established once and for all, but that which history has destined him to be *(das ihm von der Geschichte geschickte),* on the basis of which the being of man is a being-possible, constitutes his human possibilities. We see then that only from the perspective of "historicity" the meaning of the facticity of human *Dasein* becomes fully intelligible.[122]

It was *Heidegger* who carried the speculation on the nature of history to its ultimate consequences. He made it possible for us to understand the revolutionary implications of the evolution of the historical consciousness and to realize that in order to provide a philosophical foundation for this evolution it would be necessary *to break down the traditional ontology.* For this latter rested on the presupposition of the enduring and unchangeable nature of things, so that everything actual and factual appeared merely as an indifferent and accidental realization of this nature, a realization which could not possibly add anything that was essentially new and worthy of being cognitively known. From the time of antiquity the concept of philosophy had been determined as *episteme* (science, *Wissenschaft*), on the presupposed conviction that only the enduring nature of things—their truth considered as an unchangeable essence—could constitute the object of true knowledge. It follows from this premise that there can be no scientifically and philosophically relevant knowledge of the factual-historical. But the question as to the "scientific character" *(Wissenschaftlichkeit)* of the "cultural sciences"—which, after all, are in the last analysis dealing with the factual-historical—cannot be answered as long as historical structures are understood as realizations of enduring universal essences—as realizations of universal ideally "normative" values, to use the phraseology of the South-West German School. We can see therefore that *the goal of establishing a philosophic foundation of the "cultural sciences" cannot be attained without a new ontology,* an ontology which is no longer the traditional Western "ontology of essences" (*Wesensontologie*) [123] but which in all earnestness accepts the validity of the saying that the essence of human *Dasein* lies in the facticity of its existence. Only with this admission can the chief characteristic of all historical disciplines—namely, that they are sciences of the individual, the particular, and the unique—receive an historical foundation and justification. But this is only, as it were, a scientific-theoretical side-effect, while the true philosophic significance of this changed perspective lies in the fact that it places in the center of all intellectual endeavor the historicity of man's being-in-the-world and therewith the historicity of the world as such. This puts an end to the efforts of the modern age to regard man as a being who knowingly can acquire full self-mastery or absolute autonomy and—by virtue of his own power—can shape and determine the physiognomy of his own epoch. The way is thus prepared for the insight that the more modestly conceived meaning of all knowledge is the growing self-understanding of man in his particular historical situation and his self-disclosure, with a view to those demands of his situation in which a *history of Being* begins to manifest itself. This history of Being intimates what constitutes his particular situation in particular historical moments, and he is bound to conform himself more or less to these exigencies. His behavior is thus not a freely chosen projecting and planning but rather a service rendered to the "destined course of Being" (*Geschick des Seins*).

Heidegger does not mean to suggest that the "history of Being" could become the object of speculative knowledge. If this were the case, knowledge would again have to submit to the grip of human reason. Heidegger rather seems to intimate that his references to the "destiny of Being" and the "history of Being" should be understood as pointing toward an attitude which behooves man, an attitude which makes him willing to accept all that happens to him as something which is ultimately not subject to his command, so that he should not and actually cannot arrogate to himself the power to master it by speculative thinking. This intimation, must, on the other hand, not be taken as permitting the creation of an *asylum ignorantiae:* it must not lead to a renunciation of the attempt to elucidate the contexture of historical becoming with its internal logic, at least in proportion to the methodological means available to provide guidance on the road back to actual human behavior and its consequences. Heidegger himself has given us important suggestions—suggestions which we shall have yet to examine in detail—for an understanding of the contexture of the history of the West.[124] His references to the "destiny of Being" merely want to remind us to reflect on the limits of such an understanding, and he wants to emphasize that in the last analysis the facticity of the historical remains an impenetrable mystery.

Hans Freyer's imposing design of a "World History of Europe" (*Weltgeschichte Europas*) [125] rests on Heidegger's conception of historicity. It is his aim to understand the present structure of Europe as resulting from factual decisions which cannot be derived from certain given conditions, and to elucidate the meaning of the most crucial and essential among these decisions, beginning with the pre-historical stages. Hand in hand with his historical presentation he reflects philosophically on the guiding principles that were at work, so that his historiographical survey acquires the weighty significance of a European philosophy of history. Freyer's work demonstrates conclusively that the aforementioned concept of historicity does not denote an abstract philosophic program but discloses new avenues that lead to a more profound understanding of actual and factual history.

The following consequences for the concept of philosophy as such derive from Heidegger's concept of history: Since man's "finding-himself in his historical situation" always implies already a certain kind of understanding and therewith a specific interpretation of the demands implicit in this situation, the insight into these relationships posits also a definite goal for the historical inquiry into philosophy and into the function it serves in the history of human *Dasein.* This saves the history of philosophy from being dissolved in some kind of typology. Philosophy thus ceases to appear as merely one objectivation of the spirit among others. The philosophic systems are then seen as the loci where man's self-understanding in his situation acquires conceptual expression and precision. The "spirit" of different epochs manifests itself most articulately in these philosophic systems and can thus be conceptually grasped and strictly defined. Dilthey's goal of a "history of mind and spirit" thus acquires its strict methodological precision and loses the non-compelling nature of a comparative survey which is bound to become forgetful of the necessary relativity of its perspective with respect to a standpoint that is determined by the historian's own situation. The investigations carried on by Heidegger and his followers show how this historical contemplation of history must proceed and how it makes it possible to understand the history of the West —that is, our own history, which until now was guided by the ancient and traditional concept of knowledge—in its unity and in the inherent logic of its evolution. These investigations show furthermore that this understanding presupposes a breaking down of the limitations of this concept of knowledge and leads to a new definition of the meaning of knowledge. This new approach signalizes an attempt to overcome the idea that "knowledge is power" and thus tries to uncover the roots of the "crisis" of the modern age by understanding it as "the crisis of nihilism." The inquiry into the nature of history leads thus to the inquiry into the meaning of knowledge and its relationship to action.

But before we turn to a discussion of these problems, we shall try to show how in the process of a re-definition of the nature of man and of a revolutionary reversal of the traditional tenets of philosophy *the problem of art,* too, is seen in a new light and how new perspectives are leading us far beyond the traditional frame of the modern philosophy of art.

CHAPTER V

The Philosophic Problem of Art

Seventy years ago, Dilthey wrote in his essay on "The Imaginative Power of the Poet" (*Die Einbildungskraft des Dichters*): [126] "An anarchy of artistic taste is prevalent in times when a new mode of experiencing reality has shattered the existing forms and rules and when new forms of art are emerging. But this anarchy must never be allowed to endure, and it is one of the most vital tasks of contemporary philosophy as well as of the history of art and literature to restore the healthy relationship between aesthetic thinking and art." In this connection Dilthey points to the increasing power of public taste and opinion and the will of the masses. He says that art has become democratic "like everything else around us, and the thirst for reality, for solid scientific truth is alive in art too." These statements refer specifically to the growth of Naturalism, an art form in which the artists experience a new "harmony with a changed society." At the same time the educated members of society—who are, after all, the standard bearers of art theories—are still guided by an educational ideal which can be traced back to German classicism and its aesthetic canon. And since the new art no longer adheres to this ideal, Dilthey regards it as his task to restore the harmony between aesthetic thought and the actual and vital contemporary forms of art, that is, to overcome "the unproductive aesthetics which is no longer in tune with the ideas and ideals of the present age."

If we ask ourselves whether in the meantime Dilthey's demand has been fulfilled, it becomes immediately evident that this is not the case. But this is not the fault of aesthetics; it has far deeper reasons. If we want to understand the present situation with respect to the philosophic reflection on art, we must contrast it with the situation that prevailed in Dilthey's time. What has become questionable today is no longer merely the harmony of aesthetic theory and the actual and vital present art forms but the entire realm of art as such. And it is impossible to discuss the philosophy of art without taking cognizance of this changed situation. For it is this changed situation which poses genuine problems and tasks for philosophic reflection, and we shall have to show in what manner philosophic reflection is seeking to resolve these problems and fulfill these tasks.

All the art theories of the past received their directives from exemplary art works and art movements. The latter provided the unquestioned standards and norms which served as infallible guideposts for the development of art theory. This kind of guidepost is in most instances missing today. The exemplary work or the exemplary art movement which could be regarded as an unmistakably authentic expression of "a novel experience of reality" does not exist today unless we refer to the never uncontested claims of individual artists or relatively small cliques. The "anarchy of taste" has thus deeper roots than at the time when Dilthey wrote his essay; and this present day anarchy does not derive from a non-congruity of aesthetic theory and actually prevalent art forms but rather from the fact that today a predominant artistic style does not exist and that the claim of art to play an essential role in present day existence is either contested or rejected. The reason for this is to be found not only in the general turbulence of the age—"the noise of arms silences the muses" —but in the way modern man understands *Dasein*. This new conception of *Dasein* makes it impossible for art to occupy an important position. If it is true, however, that this new understanding of *Dasein* is determined by the predominance of a technological world-interpretation, and if it is the task of philosophy to overcome this technological world view, the philosophic inquiry into the nature of art, too, must proceed within the same horizon and must be understood in the same sense. It will then be seen that art is not to serve a special clique of "esthetes" but has to fulfill an essential function.

As much as it would seem inappropriate to measure art, for example, by the standard of its more or less "proletarian" character, such a demand expresses nonetheless—albeit in a perverted form—a well founded desire to re-unite art and life. Such a reunion is mandatory if art is to retain any justification to exist in a world which is determined by the concept of labor and by the power of technology. In other words, the standard of measurement must be gained from the relatedness of art to actual and factual human *Dasein*. In this way even those manifest aberrations of thinking which have made all contemporary art appear questionable, can acquire positive significance: they offer an elementary philosophic challenge to art, and they may thus lead to the insight that *prior to all aesthetic questions the question as to the values of truth inherent in art must be answered*. This question as to the nature and the truth of art has not only not been answered adequately by philosophy since the time of German Idealism but it has even been completely lost sight of. Only at a time when an exemplary art which—as an unquestioned given entity—could provide a standard of measurement for all artistic creation—was lacking, did it become once more possible to realize that every aesthetics must be preceded by a metaphysics of art. Only at that moment could art as such become problematical; for, notwithstanding the non-existence of an exemplary artistic model, art as such did not simply fade from the horizon. There still remained the claim—no matter how much contested—of modern art to due recognition, and there also remained the no less contested values of the traditional art of the past as embodied in literature, music, painting, as exhibited in libraries, museums, and concert halls. And there remained finally the ever repeated question as to what it is that imparts to these works of the past their lasting effect, the question whether these creations were merely the by-products of a relaxation from a life of hard labor or whether they had some deeper significance. It became increasingly clear that this question could not be answered by aesthetics and by a theory of art.

To explain the reasons for this failure to arrive at a satisfactory answer, we must look at *the origin of this incongruity between aesthetics and art theory, on the one hand, and the metaphysics of art, on the other*. And we must try to elucidate the meaning of this contrariety. We can understand the problems of contemporary art only by viewing from an historical point of view the original bases of those philosophic questions with which art had to contend. If we do this, we shall find that the kind of questioning was determined by these historical origins almost to this present day and that it will be necessary to rid ourselves gradually from this more or less latent predetermination.

The contrast between aesthetics and metaphysics is already implicit in the very beginnings of the philosophic speculation on the nature of art, within the circumference of the Western tradition. Even then *the beautiful was*—once and for all—*determined as the object of art,* and this determination marked the origin of *the strained relations that exist between the beautiful* (that is, the basic problem of art theory) and the true (that is, the basic problem of the metaphysics of art). Already Plato's philosophy poses—without making art its special theme—the basic problem that must of necessity be posed in any philosophy of art, namely, the question as to the truth content and the truth value of art. Within the frame of the query concerning the truth which man needs in order to learn what he ought to do, art—which up to that time had been the unchallenged teacher of the Greeks—became a problem. The formative process which leads to human perfection, to the realization of the genuinely human—the acquisition and possession of "virtue"—is for Plato tied to the contemplation of the Ideas and to the graduated evolution of educative formation. In the course of this development the "good" comes to be understood as the specific perfection which each and every thing and being must possess in order to be truly what it is. At the apex of this graduated scale Plato placed the Idea of the Good as such which makes possible the goodness or the "being-good" of each and every individual thing and being. In this gradual ascent toward the contemplation of truth, therefore, art can be assigned its proper place, and the individual arts can be examined to find out to what extent they can serve this ascent. Although the truth of philosophic knowledge is here placed above that truth which is embodied in art within the realm of sensorial appearance, art retains nonetheless in this graduated scale its definitive place in the contexture of Greek education and civilization. And whenever and wherever in later periods the question concerning the truth of art is asked, it always remains within the same frame of reference. This happens, for example, in the period of Enlightenment, especially since Shaftesbury, where the emphasis is placed on the pedagogical function of art in the cultivation of "feeling"—an idea which is later on stressed by Lessing and Schiller—or again, in the case of Hegel, who sees in the beautiful the sensorial appearance of the Idea. Moving in the same direction, *Konrad Fiedler* finally tried to determine the nature of art as "a knowledge of those means by which man first gains holds of reality." He wanted to place art in the service of education and thus initiated, on the one hand, the movement of art education in Germany while, on the other, he tried to protect the idea of artistic truth from that narrowness which threatened from the creed of Naturalism.

By the side of *this philosophy of art—which regarded art as a potent educational force*—stood since Aristotle a *theory of art* which was not—as it was in Plato's philosophy—a metaphysics of the beautiful but rather a theory of *poiesis,* a theory of the creation of beautiful works. From then on the theory of art assumed the character of *a theory of artistic creation,* its rules and its norms. The contrast of this kind of theory to philosophy becomes fully evident when we call to mind Shaftesbury's conviction that the "really beautiful" is not that which is beautifully made but rather that which makes beautiful or that which imparts beauty. As against this Platonically inspired conviction, the theory of art remains an inseparable companion of artistic activity, especially in the period of the Renaissance when almost all creative artists were simultaneously theoreticians of art.

When, with Descartes, philosophic thought was centered exclusively in the subject, this theory received a new twist. This change was initiated in large part by *Shaftesbury* and *Leibniz*. Now the query concerns no longer only the rules of the creation of works of art, but the subject as their producer or creator moves into the center of the theoretic speculation —the inquiry into those psychical faculties of the artist which are responsible for both the creation and the receptive appreciation of works of art. This marks the beginnings of the modern development of aesthetics, an aesthetics which is essentially *a theory of the productive-creative aesthetic faculty*. The foundation was laid by the aesthetics of *Baumgarten* which treats especially of operations of the lower, that is, the sensorial-aesthetic faculties.

It was *Kant* who once more integrated aesthetics in the total structure of philosophy by assigning to the feelings of "pleasure" (*Lust*) and "displeasure" (*Unlust*) an intermediate position between knowing and willing and by inquiring into the underlying a priori principles of taste. He defined the beautiful—the object of a "disinterested pleasure"—as *a symbol of morality*. He thereby took an important step forward not only in aesthetics but in the development of the philosophy of art and the inquiry into its true nature—an advance which came to its fruition in philosophic Idealism. The concept of the "genius" became now of central significance, in Kant's own time as well as in subsequent speculation. In the inquiry into the nature of "genius" the subjective trend of the philosophy of art reached its peak. Genius was defined, above all else, as the actualization of the aesthetic potency, as "the talent (that is, the natural disposition) which determines the rules of art." [127]

With a breakdown of Idealism, its advance toward the development of a philosophy of art—that is, toward an overcoming of the narrowness of both the theory of artistic creation and the analysis of the psychical faculties responsible for the creative processes—was again abandoned. At this juncture it became possible for the turning of modern philosophy toward the subject to become fully effective also in the inquiry into the nature of art. The basic question of every philosophy of art—the question whether and to what extent art is a carrier of truth—is silenced from the outset by the conviction that the true is that which can be scientifically and objectively determined. This conviction relegates art to a realm of "beautiful appearance" (*schöner Schein*) and finally reduces it to a mere ornamental embellishment of life. That realm which remains reserved for aesthetics is subsequently delimited by the simultaneous abandonment of the conviction that human nature with its several faculties is an unchangeable constant. This feat was accomplished by a kind of historical thinking which was initiated by *Winckelmann's* insight that the beautiful is not a concept of timeless validity but has its own history. It is this view which delineated the paths which aesthetics has more or less followed to this day. It has moved along these paths in the two main directions of *psychological* and *historical* inquiry, that is, in the comparative study of those aesthetic values and ends which make their appearance in history and in the appraisal of their historical and sociological conditionality.[128]

If we want to understand the current status of the philosophic speculation on the nature of art, it is necessary to keep in mind the above mentioned historical premises. They provide the set of conditions which made it possible that until quite recently the philosophy of art in general was equated with aesthetics, so that the possibility of any questioning beyond this equation was no longer seen at all. But if aesthetics is willing to accept art unquestioningly as a historically given facticity that can be subjected to psychological, historical, and sociological investigation, it cannot possibly do justice to our present situation, a situation in which not merely one particular trend or one particular artistic style but art as such has become problematic. Such a situation demands a radical re-examination of the interrelationship of art and human *Dasein,* and this kind of examination transcends the boundaries of any aesthetics. Only by an historical elucidation of the origination of the boundaries of aesthetics in the modern philosophy of the subject, with its dichotomy of an "internal" and an objective "external" world, can the still prevalent and exclusively dominant problematics of aesthetics be understood. Such an understanding will also reveal the reasons for the dissatisfaction which this kind of investigation carries in its wake. This is why *any attempt to develop a philosophy of art on a different set of premises must start out from a reflection on the history of the problems relating to this kind of philosophy*. And it must aim at revealing and eventually overcoming the hidden historical presuppositions which are still determining modern thought, so that at long last the speculation on the nature of art can be brought in line with the genuine problems of our present age. This kind of reflection must of necessity also result in a *destruction* of the established traditions of the philosophy of art and of aesthetics. This follows of necessity as the final step in the development of the historical consciousness.[129]

In view of this situation it becomes understandable why, for example, the article *Ästhetik* by *Alfred Baeumler* (in *Handbuch der Philosophie*) is not more than an historical introduction in which the author, in presenting the dualism of the metaphysics of beauty and the theory of art (aesthetics) as "the secret law of the entire historical evolution" (p. 85), demands that one has recourse to the changing central metaphysical concepts in order to gain insight into the changing artistic styles and into the nature of art as such (p. 35). For the limitations of a psychologically and sociologically oriented aesthetics can be transcended only when a historical reflection can demonstrate that even the supposedly purely empirical and unmetaphysical aesthetic investigations are guided by hidden metaphysical presuppositions. These hidden presuppositions derive from the modern philosophy of the subject with its implicit correlative notion of an "objective" truth. In this situation philosophic reflection finds itself confronted with a task which presents a close parallel to the tasks which the previously discussed fields and disciplines had to face.

In the following pages we shall have to review the steps which were taken to break away from the domineering force of the aesthetic tradition and to prepare the way for a new kind of inquiry into the nature of art.

Two principal points of departure must be noted because they determine the direction which the reflection on the nature of art has been following in our own time. The first is Dilthey's *Poetik,* the second Husserl's analysis of "expression" and "significant meaning" (*Bedeutung*) in his "Logical Investigations" (*Logische Untersuchungen,* 1900-1901).

Dilthey understood the task he was facing—as it appeared to him within the horizon of his age—as a re-formation of aesthetics which was to make it possible to do justice to the new developments in art and to elaborate the categories by means of which these developments could be adequately understood. The superficial observer might conclude that Dilthey's investigations proceeded within the frame of this task in that they were trying to resolve the inherent problem by means of a psychological analysis of those inward experiences which find their expression in the work of art. He speaks in this sense of a "psychological elementary doctrine of poetry." [130] It is only when one adds to these early investigations on *Poetik* his later research—in which he delves more deeply [131] into the meaning of "inward experience" by a regress to the "efficient contexture" (*Wirkungszusammenhang*) of the historical world—that it becomes evident that his perspectives had from the outset been broader than the "objectivism" which had been taken for granted throughout the nineteenth century. Dilthey himself was at the beginning not fully conscious of the implications and consequences of his new approach. It became clear now that the inwardly experiencing subjectivity could no longer be understood as a subject shut up in himself and finding himself opposed by an "objective world" but that the subject—embedded in the "efficient contexture of history"—is merely the crossing-point of historical forces, a focal point of energy which provides a proper setting for "vital feeling" (*Lebensgefühl*) and for the basic "life-moods" to disclose and comprehend the nature of reality. And this new kind of comprehensive understanding is then no longer a passive acceptance of an already existing reality "in-itself" but rather the lowest formative principle of all reality, the principle which makes it possible for reality to become articulate.

New light is thus cast on the function of poetry. Dilthey turned against "the artificial attempt to separate the beautiful from the experiences of life" because it sees the function of poetry in a mere embellishment of reality. He points out that the process of artistic creation is not autonomous in the sense that it proceeds aside from the everyday understanding of reality, but it rather signifies an intensification of what occurs in all ordinary everyday experience. "It is true that images and their combinations transcend the ordinary experiences of life, but whatever comes into being [in the creative process] represents these same experiences, contributing to a more profound understanding and a more inward appropriation." [132] Dilthey thus attributes to the work of art *the function of being not a subsequent interpretation of a previously experienced reality but rather an exemplary project of this reality itself.* He thereby establishes as the general principle of all artistic creation the "ideality" of art, that is, the thesis that art is not merely a replica or a reduplication of a given reality but an intensification of reality, a profilization of the essential and most significant features of reality. According to Dilthey, it is the function of art and of artistic creation to teach us to see reality, and it is therefore the genius, that is, the creative individual, who in his experiences realizes to the fullest extent that intensification which makes possible the productive-creative expression. "In religion and philosophy as well as in art, and especially in poetry, the coordination of constitutive parts . . . to form a unity which transcends that which is given, is brought about by an historical creative process. In this way that unity which we call the spirit of an age is being formed by the creative genius out of originally very manifold constitutive parts and their multiple interrelation." [133] However, the genius—and this is the deep meaning which Dilthey imparted to this traditional concept—is not to be understood in his individuality as an intensified and heightened subjectivity, as the exception that unfathomably and inexplicably breaks into the historical evolution but rather as a "crossing-point" (*Kreuzungspunkt*) in the historical conjunction of efficacious events, a being in whom the historical forces have become incarnate, in whom they have been digested as well as intensified. This, to be sure, results in the breaking of traditional horizons, in a manner that cannot be calculated on the basis of any given facticities, so that eventually the spirit of a newly rising epoch is actualized for the first time. There exists then a reciprocal efficacity between art and everyday life: art results from a heightened intensification of life and in its turn reacts efficaciously on life by illumining for a historical epoch its guiding ideals and aspirations, in the form of images rather than—as is the case in philosophy—in the form of concepts. In this sense poetry "makes visible the meaning and significance of life": it is a representation of life in the form of poetic images. And poetry is not merely one representation among others but—after the collapse of a universally binding religious foundation of life—it fulfills a preeminent function in making visible what it is that moves and motivates the individuals of an epoch in their innermost being. "Since religion has lost its hold on the metaphysical demonstration of the existence of God and the soul, a large number of our contemporaries can find an ideal understanding of the meaning of life only in art and poetry." [134]

Even though this statement was made with reference to the ideas underlying the education and culture prevalent at the end of the nineteenth century and is hardly any longer valid for our own time, it should be recognized that this interpretation of the nature of art embodies a new principle that transcends in its significance the limiting conditions of that particular epoch. This new principle does not only combine the psychological and the historical points of view,[135] but it simultaneously imparts a new and deeper meaning to the question concerning the interrelation between the art forms and the total intellectual physiognomy of a period. This new meaning points beyond the narrow schema of substructure and superstructure [136] as well as beyond the schema of a relativistic perspective which merely inquires into the historical conditions that underlie certain types of art and artists and their sociological determination by the given facticities of their age. The new principle contains implicitly a new philosophic predication regarding the nature of art and its significance for life, a predication which opens up new horizons within which the activities of life proceed and unfold. However, this kind of predication concerning the meaning and significance of life is peculiar to the language of art and cannot be made by any other expressive mode of life. The manifestation of life's meaning and significance in the form of artistic and poetic images and in the uniqueness of a historical situation is an *original disclosure of reality*—original in the sense that it precedes all reflection and intellectual-rational analysis and extends into that dimension of "life-moods" which underlies all articulations of reality. This dimension, rightly understood, denotes exactly what *Heidegger* has in mind when he speaks of the "mood" or "state-of-mind" (*Befindlichkeit*) of human *Dasein*.

The new approach to the interpretation of art and literature initiated by Dilthey eventually led—in contrast to the positivistically and biographic-psychologically oriented history of art and literature prevalent during the final decades of the nineteenth century—to a presentation from the point of view of the "History of Ideas" (*Geistesgeschichte*), that is, to an attempt to regard the individual works in their historical context as expressions of the spirit of an epoch. The effects of Dilthey's "new look" at art and literature were especially far reaching in the field of literary criticism (*Literaturwissenschaft*).[137] Dilthey's ideas on art and literature were embodied impressively in the research of his pupil, *Hermann Nohl,* who applied them to the special problems of contemporary pedagogy and general education.[138]

Dilthey's approach signalized moreover *the abandonment of all attempts at psychological explications and a turning toward an analysis of the works themselves.* The individual work itself and its structural laws—which are related to that psychical context which in its turn is causally related to the context of the historical world and its situational facticity—moves once again into the center of attention and consideration. This decisive change of view was aided by the second important point of departure of the contemporary philosophy of art, that is, by Husserl's "Logical Investigations," which subjected to close analysis the nature of "expression" and "meaning." Husserl's "re-formation" of logic, which led to its liberation from the fetters of psychologism, laid the foundation for a recognition of the ideal unity of significant meaning as against the manifoldness of the subjective experiences in which this unity of meaning is actualized. This emphasis on "ideality" gave also a new direction to the critical appreciation of works of art as ideal unities, as pure essences. *Roman Ingarden* subjected the nature of the literary work of art to close scrutiny and contrasted it with other linguistic structures.[139] *Max Scheler,* in turn, integrated the critical analysis of the work of art as an ideal unity with his metaphysics of "actualized values" and their dynamic structure, a structure which includes both ideal and real factors.[140] On the other hand, it may be observed that all these investigations do not take account of Dilthey's principal thesis which posited the work of art as an objectivation of life and demanded that it be understood as such on the basis of the historical cause-and-effect context, so that on this same basis the main problem of the philosophy of art—the problem of the specific nature of artistic and poetic truth—might be resolved. This problem is now approached from the perspective of a supra-temporal "intuition of essences" (*Wesensschau*). However, the problems formulated by Dilthey are being taken up and are being posed in a more radical form by a fairly large numer of other investigations and investigators.

In this development the writings of *Moritz Geiger,* which took their start from Husserl's phenomenological method, occupy a peculiar kind of intermediate position. Although the problems discussed by Geiger—beginning with an analysis of aesthetic pleasure [141]—seem to remain wholly within the frame of the subjectivism of modern aesthetics, he raises several questions which pierce this narrow frame and seem to point toward a metaphysical answer, an answer, however, which Geiger himself did never give explicitly and methodoligally. When Geiger, for example, distinguishes in a careful analysis between "external concentration"—an attitude which he deems alone adequate for the reception and appreciation of a work of art—and "internal concentration," he thereby undermines the vulgar idea of the nature of aesthetic pleasure, considered as an attitude which does not "enter into" the work but rather expects to be stimulated by it or to be swayed into a subjectively conditioned "mood." Hand in hand with this goes a critique of the "theory of empathy" (*Einfühlungstheorie*) which, since *Theodor Lipps* and *Wilhelm Worringer* first coined the term, has become a kind of catch-word. To approach the work with "empathy" cannot possibly mean to "enter into" the inwardness of the artist who has created a particular work but rather to gain entrance into the artist's world-view, that is, to enter into his manner of seeing the world and its objects.[142] The genuinely aesthetic attitude must therefore be willing to be led by the work itself. It is this attitude which lifts us out of the perspective of ordinary everyday life to the level of "existential qualitative contemplation." [143] This point of view implies that the essential significance of the work of art for the discovery and penetration of reality is recognized. Geiger's references to cult and ornament as two sources of artistic creation—references which might well have led him to appreciate the interrelation of art and the festive elevation and transfiguration of life—are unfortunately not further elaborated. For if he had wanted to base this interrelationship on a philosophic foundation, in order to make visible the meaning and significance of truth in relation to art, he would have had to abandon the objective-scientific concept of truth. And he would have been compelled to revise or reverse the order which prevails between cognition as a tool in the service of life, on the one hand, and the disclosure of the truth of Being, on the other. For this disclosure is more than a mere operative function in the service of life.[144]

Further steps in the direction toward a metaphysics of art were taken by *Fritz Kaufmann,* in his analysis of artistic "mood." [145] He grounds Dilthey's concept of "life-mood" in a new depth-dimension and thus arrives with *Heidegger* at the notion of "being-in-a-mood" (*Gestimmtsein*), regarded as the fundamental "state-of-mind" (*Grundbefindlichkeit*) of human *Dasein* which discloses or reveals the world in its totality. The work of art, to be sure, is always a representation of an individuality, but precisely as such it is above all the expression of a "life-mood." It permits us to see the individual within the total context of his world. The standard of measurement for the truth of a work of art is therefore not a "correctness" that can be gauged by the criterion of objectivity but rather the "depth" of the work, that is, the mode and manner of its world-disclosure—world understood in the previously discussed sense.[146]

The two methods of analysis—the one guided by the problem of the ideality of expression (*Ingarden*), the other by the problem of "mood" (*Kaufmann*)—are combined in the writings of *Johannes Pfeiffer*.[147] In an analysis which is centered in an investigation of the nature of lyric poetry, Pfeiffer explains—both generally and with specific application to the interpretation of individual works—how the structural form of the work of art results from the musical elements in the expressive media. He wants to show "what poetry is in its essence and how this essence is grounded in our human life and in *Dasein* as a whole." Aside from the beauty that derives from the formative power, and aside from the truth which rests on the "power of illumination" (*Erhellungskraft*), the work of art has a "power of appeal." With this phrase—which calls to mind the terminology of *Karl Jaspers*[148]—the humanizing function of art is, as in Platonism, once again of central significance, and the perspective of interpretation is that of the *Philosophy of Existence*. But Pfeiffer is convinced that both philosophic knowledge with its potential "power of appeal" and art fall short of religious certitude and cannot provide substitutes for the latter.

While Pfeiffer's writings show the possibilities inherent in an analysis of "moods," of "states-of-mind," *Emil Staiger* starts out from an even more deeply grounded complex of problems embodied in Heidegger's *Daseins-analysis,* namely, from the structures of "temporality." He too does not formulate new theories but attempts to make visible the different modes in which "temporality" is experienced. He does so by showing the innermost structural principle of individual poems, by means of exemplary interpretation.[149] Even further leads his attempt at writing a new "poetics," [150] in which the differences between the three basic forms of poetry—lyric, epic, drama—are derived from the three different dimensions of "temporality." It would lead us too far afield if we tried to discuss the objections which might be raised against Staiger's attempt. The main objection is based on the fact that Staiger's "forms of poetry" are seen by him too much as timeless types, that he disregards the historical origin and the historical determination which are to some extent incarnate in all such ideal "types." But despite these possible and perhaps necessary objections, it remains Staiger's merit to have been the first one in our time who on a new foundation has presented for discussion the ancient problem of the "categorial forms of poetry" (*Dichtungsarten*).

Aside from these writings which are trying to approach the basic philosophic problems of poetry analytically, there are projects aiming at a metaphysics of art. Among these *Oskar Becker's* essay "on the Caducity of the Beautiful and the Adventurousness of the Artist" [151] deserves special mention. Using the categories of Heidegger's "existential ontology" (*Existentialontologie*), Becker traces the work of art in its fragility back to a fulfilled moment of *Dasein,* a moment which is embodied in the work in its "eternal" validity. The "thrownness" (*Geworfenheit*) of *Dasein* in its historical facticity [152] is absorbed, preserved and sustained in the individual work of art. The "adventurousness" of the artist manifests itself in the fact that he is capable of keeping a precarious balance on that brink where the uniqueness and the eternity of the fulfilled moment fuse in the perfection of the work of art. The artist thus transcends and annuls the temporality of a *Dasein* which is always "ahead of itself" (*Sichvorwegsein*) in its anticipation (*Vorlaufen*) of death. However, Becker's attempted broadening of certain ideas which Heidegger discussed in "Being and Time" (*Sein und Zeit*) is not developed into a metaphysics of art.

Kurt Riezler, on the other hand, making use of Heidegger's categories, consciously attempted to develop a metaphysics of art.[153] He tried to derive the possbility of artistic creation and the nature of the beautiful from an analysis of *Dasein's* temporality and spatiality. *"Physis,"* according to Heraclitus, "likes to hide. Between its edges (*Fugen*), pulled roughly from precipice to precipice, staggers the blind human being, concealed to himself. And yet the hidden structure is present and manifest in the whole, determining what each individual entity 'is' and remaining concealed in its very presence." That which—in art—causes a thing or being to be "good," depends on the measure of the visibility to which the individual structure attains on its way from concealedness to manifest overtness. In short, the individual work of art is "transparent" with respect to the "goodness" which is incarnate in it. And it is this transparency which is the "ground" of its beauty. Beauty, in other words, is the phenomenal manifestation of the hidden goodness. This "is"—understood in the sense of saying, "a work is present" —carries the following meaning: "Something intermediate stands in between the being of the soul and the work as an object in the real world, and it is in this intermediate entity that a mysterious fusion occurs of the one with the other, of the internal with the external." [154] The individual work is not an expression of something which stands expressively behind it: it is and is simultaneous not the expressed entity. That which shines in the work and which "in its shining is already past, compels art to speak—at the moment of an inspiration in which both the artist and the observing spectator share. Perhaps not only the observing spectator but also the one who tries to enunciate the mystery of the good in philosophic language, have need of this inspiration. The latter has perhaps intuited this mystery in a fleeting fulfilled moment, but it has disappeared while he was trying to enunciate it." [155] Riezler thus elaborates further Becker's idea of the caducity of beauty, a beauty which was fleetingly illumined in one fulfilled moment. It is the great merit of Riezler's approach to have uncovered the paradoxes which attach to any ontology that takes its orientation from thingly reality, if we make an attempt to determine the *Dasein* of the work of art—that is, of what the work of art is "in truth"—by means of such an ontology.

This same problem occupies the center of Heidegger's essay on "The Origin of the Work of Art" (*Der Ursprung des Kunstwerkes* [in *Holzwege*]). Insight into the origin, that is, into the aboriginal essence of the work of art and into the nature or essence of art itself can be gained only by demolishing the traditional aesthetic-theoretical conceptual edifice. And since these concepts themselves grew out of the history of metaphysics, their destruction becomes a part-problem that is encountered on "the road back to the ground of metaphysics." [156] There is no doubt that traditional philosophic thought is unable to answer the question as to the quiddity of a thing (*was ein Ding ist*) because, owing to the tyrannical rule of the logic of predication, the structure of any affirmative proposition—as a linkage of subject and predicate—was projected into the structure of the object, the latter being understood as a union of substance and accidents. And there was also the second possibility, namely, to regard the production-schema of the "equipment" (*das Zeug*) as the measure to be used in the attempt to arrive at a determination of the object as a composite of form and matter. It was thus the fate of traditional aesthetics that it was always bound to apply one of these traditional schematas whenever it was a question of understanding the work of art. This means, however, *that traditional ontology can in none of its forms—and whatever interpretation may be attempted —serve as a guide to the understanding of the nature of the art work as such*. For this nature abides in a dimension which is disregarded by traditional metaphysics and ontology from the beginning to the end. What kind of dimension is this? It is the dimension of either the self-disclosure or the self-concealment of Being. Only by paying heed to this dimension can the "reposing-in-itself" (*das In-sich-Ruhen*) of the work of art be understood. It is in the self-disclosure or self-concealment of Being that the world of *Dasein* opens up. And it is of the very essence of the work of art that it opens up and keeps open an historical world as the stage upon which the *Dasein* of a people or a nation is being enacted. The work of art is essentially productive-creative (*herstellend*). "The temple-structure, by producing a world, does not cause matter to disappear but, on the contrary, makes it appear in opening up the world of the work: the rock becomes carrier and repose and thus becomes truly rock; the metals begin to flash and glimmer, the colors begin to gleam and sparkle, the tones begin to ring out, the word begins to speak." Only in the work itself becomes visible what weight is, what a word is, what a tone is. "Matter," "stuff" and, in the last analysis, "the earth" have not disappeared: "the work of art moves the earth into the overtness of a world and maintains it in overtness." [157] The "workmanship" (*das Werksein*) of a work of art is thus "one of the modes of truth becoming incarnate (*wie Wahrheit geschieht*). Setting up a world and firmly 'placing' the earth, the work of art is a 'contesting' (*Bestreitung*) of that contest in which the 'unconcealedness' (*Unverborgenheit*) of all that which is in its totality (*des Seienden im Ganzen*)—that is, truth—is conquered as the prize of the contest." In this sense then "the 'realization of the work' (*das Werkwerden des Werkes*) is a mode of the becoming and the incarnation of truth." Scientific knowledge, on the other hand, "is not an original incarnation of truth (*Geschehen der Wahrheit*) but always merely the elaboration of an already overt realm of truth." [158]

These philosophic reflections of Heidegger see art in a perspective that is wider than that of Plato's inquiry into the truth of art, broader than that complex of problems centering in the "humanistic" education of man [159] which to this day has secretly dominated every philosophy of art. Heidegger's perspective extends also far beyond the problems of any traditional theory of art and aesthetics. The work of art stands here side by side with the work of the thinker. According to Heidegger, it is the "poets and thinkers" who in their "speaking" (*Sagen*) are the original builders of a world. Heidegger's interpretation of Hölderlin's poetry aims at this original meaning of "speaking." This implies the demand of a reversal of our thinking habits, according to which we are used to understand speech and language as tools of communication and as means of expressing the thoughts of human subjects. This attitude presupposes that what is "first" is subjects and their "inward experiences" which are subsequently expressed and communicated. This relationship must be reversed: we must become aware of the fact that the subjects do not "first" have experiences which make it possible for them to express their thoughts and to listen to those who address them, but the subjects are capable of having inner experiences because they are "first" listening to the claim and address of Being. What makes possible the freedom of man as an experiencing and expressively self-revelatory subject is a "being-able-to-hear," understood as overtness for the address of Being. The works of poets and thinkers must therefore not be understood as free expressions of human subjectivity, as expressions of their thinking. That freedom which underlies the possibility of expression is rather the stage or place where the truth of Being is revealed. Freedom is thus overtness for a hearkening to the aboriginal truth of Being (in the sense of the Greek *aletheia,* that is, unconcealedness, re-velation), as it speaks through the mouths of poets and thinkers. These latter are the mediators of what Being has to say to man, and they create in their speaking the space in which different epochs attain to self-understanding. In this speaking "a world is being produced." The "mittence of Being" (*Geschick des Seins*)*—that which Being "com-missions" man to be—forms the basis of an understanding of the works of art in their historicity. The striving for an intellectual and spiritual understanding of history (*geistesgeschichtliches Verständnis*), inaugurated by Dilthey, is thus rooted in a philosophy of Being. But such a philosophy of Being became possible only after the demolition of the edifice of Western metaphysics and after the modern subjectivism of art had been overcome. Only now could art as such be understood in its essential meaning and significance. We do well, however, to caution that these ideas represent little more than mere beginnings.

* The English neologisms "mittence of Being" (*Geschick des Seins*) and, in the last chapter of this book, "foundational thinking" (*wesentliches Denken*) are both adopted from William J. Richardson's probably definitive interpretation of Heidegger's thought (see *Bibliography*).

Nothing has as yet been definitely determined concerning the interrelationship of poetic and philosophic communication or as to whether poetry and philosophy are of equal rank or whether the one is to be subordinated to the other. A clarification of the nature of this interrelationship presupposes a resolution of certain fundamental problems of logic and of the philosophy of language, problems which up to now have not even been clearly formulated.

CHAPTER VI

Knowledge and Action

The preceding discussions have shown several aspects of contemporary thought which illustrate the general tendency to do away with the rigid divisions among the different philosophic disciplines. This applies also to the sphere of problems which concern human action and its relation to knowledge. Especially since Kant the separation of theoretical and practical philosophy—of epistemology as a foundation of scientific knowledge and ethics as an inquiry into the norms of action, in correlation with an axiology which was to furnish the principles from which these norms are derived—had been taken for granted. Today philosophy is on its way to regain sight of the unity of these problems, a unity which was a decisive and essential ingredient at the very beginnings of Western philosophy. For since the time when—with Socrates and Plato—philosophy turned from the problems of cosmology to the inquiry into the nature of man, the function of philosophy was thought to consist in bringing about the formation of man's true nature or essence. Regardless of whether philosophic knowledge was understood Platonically as a beholding of the Ideas or—from the Christian point of view—as an either intellectual-rational or intuitive perception of the order of creation, the conviction always prevailed that this kind of knowledge imparts to man certainty regarding the norms according to which he has to orient his actions. Philosophic-scientific knowledge of the world and its order was separated from the question concerning the possibilities of action and the means of arriving at guiding norms of action only owing to the modern conviction of the "objectivity" of an "external" world-in-itself. a world of which it was believed that it could be known—without any presuppositions—by theoretical science. Man's freedom, in which the potentialities of his being as an acting entity are rooted, ceased to be a problem of theoretical knowledge. This meant also that from the knowledge of the objective world no consequences whatever could be derived with respect to the norms of human action and with respect to those values which form the bases of these norms. Knowledge "without presuppositions" (*Voraussetzungslosigkeit*) and "abstention from value judgments" (*Wertfreiheit*) were proclaimed as the two fundamental principles of strict science.[160] The "realm of values" was thus opposed to the reality of worldly being, and the attempt was made to define the former as a realm of supra-temporal, ideal axiological norms.

This then was the basic position of philosophy at the end of the nineteenth and the beginning of the twentieth century. *The separation of being and value,* which had been more or less covertly assumed in the modern concept of science from the outset, was thus consummated. The "philosophy of value" understood itself as a counter-movement against the tendency toward a psychologizing relativization of values, a tendency prevalent in the nineteenth century since the breakdown of Idealism. This relativization of values has implied the reduction of values to the psychical and psychological condition and disposition of man—his strivings and desires, which were supposed to determine the standard of all his values. The historical consciousness had gained insight into the relativity of theoretical world views as well as of the prevalent valuations and norms with respect to the particular historical structure of an epoch. In view of this twofold relativization, the philosophers tried to salvage the absoluteness of these valuations and norms by relegating them to a realm of supra-temporal validity. As against this kind of relativization and especially against Nietzsche's "devaluation of all traditional values," they regarded it as the task of philosophy to stress the universal validity of the so-called "cultural values." [161] In short, it was argued that the validity of values could not possibly have its foundation in their historical facticity and intelligibility.

At first this counter-move against the relativism of values had remained a specific problem of philosophy. However, the shattering of the optimistic cultural consciousness that occurred in the wake of the First World War created a general awareness that Europe was experiencing not only a crisis of philosophic thought but a crisis of humanity as such. It was only in the decades that followed the end of the war that Nietzsche's prophesy of the imminent advent of European Nihilism—that is, the devaluation of the highest values—could no longer be shoved aside as the idea of a strange "outsider" or a pathologically disturbed mind. The Nietzschean prophesy was fulfilled in Germany earlier than in those countries which had emerged victoriously from the First World War and which had returned to an apparent security of their national existence. It was only the crises of the third decade of our century and of the Second World War which aroused in those countries too the consciousness that Nietzsche's prophesy of the imminent advent of European Nihilism was not a poetic metaphor or a merely academic problem but *called in question the very foundations of the Western tradition and its ideals.* The questioning concerning a "renewal of the West" was now regarded as fundamental; it was a question which had to be answered by philosophy. And in trying to answer this question, philosophy had to demonstrate that it—as the one authoritative voice that remained after the ancient Christian-religious foundations of life had been badly shaken—was able to give a new "hold" or anchorage to contemporary man. What was at stake was not only the general and, as it were, timeless question concerning the establishment of the norms of human action and of the correlative guiding values and ideals but rather the question as to what philosophy might be able to contribute to this kind of "renewal." This entire question is more and more overshadowed by that kind of world-interpretation which understands human action in the sense of technological world domination and in relation to the technical processes of production. While the optimistic progressivism of the nineteenth century rested precisely on the affirmation of the fact of the steadily advancing power of technological world domination—understood as a process by means of which man takes possession of his freedom—, in our own day and age the insecurity regarding the highest norms of action has, in view of the greater immediacy of the threatening dangers, become so universal that this possibility of the dominion of technology and of modes of action which derive their norms from this supreme master-value, can easily turn against man and the realization of his freedom and may not only entail his enslavement but even his total annihilation. The "demonic" nature of technology is indicted, and the threatening picture of a mankind enslaved by the apparatus of technology is sketched not only in philosophic and semi-philosophic writings but also in prominent works of literature.

The question as to the proper human attitude, that is, the guiding ideal principles of human action, receives thus a very definite emphasis that relates it to the distress and turbulence of the present moment. The guiding norms which are to be adopted must be capable of stemming the tide of these threatening contingencies. In this connection we do well to remember that technology derives in the last analysis from the modern ideal image of science which calls for the realization of the motto, "knowledge is power," a saying which marked the birth of modern science. It was this modern concept of science which caused the separation of knowledge and action, of theoretical and practical certitude, of a realm of objective being and a realm of ideal "values." It becomes thus evident that *the problem of the "conquest of Nihilism" is inseparable from the problem as to the new meaning which the utilization of the possibilities of technological world domination may assume through the instrumentality of man.* This problem, however, cannot be resolved without a new definition of the meaning of scientific and philosophic knowledge and their relation to human action. In wrestling with this task, philosophy itself moves beyond all academic discussions of the problems of relativity and of the hierarchy of values into a dimension where out of the predicaments of the present moment a choice must be made that will be decisive for the philosophy of the future, its possibilities and its tasks.

Up to this point there is almost general agreement among the representatives of contemporary European philosophy. The question as to the "values" upon which the norms of human action ought to be based, is raised in connection with the existential problem of the "crisis of the West," a crisis which—as the crisis of the technological world view—casts its shadow over the whole world. However, there is unanimity only with respect to the problem as such, but not with respect to the possibilities of a *solution.* It is here where there prevails almost universal confusion, and the style of the answers which are being given reveals that the several points are not at all clearly seen and defined and that no one really knows where to start and against whom or what to fight. It is generally agreed, to be sure, that the traditional attempts to establish guiding values, norms, and corresponding *moral theories do no longer satisfy the demands of present day life* [162] and that for this reason they must be placed on a new foundation. To do this requires a *new orientation* with respect to the nature and the situation of man, an orientation that is freed from the schemata of the traditional philosophic systems.[163] The sources of human valuations are therefore being investigated anew,[164] with the result that one begins to see that each philosophic system presupposes a basic metaphysical position. The question as to the nature and rank of values can therefore not be answered without taking account of metaphysical presuppositions.

As we have mentioned before, the general agreement concerning the problems at hand does by no means exclude a complete divergence of convictions, as far as the proposed solutions are concerned. The latter come from many quarters: from Catholic Thomism,[165] from "Christian Existentialism," [166] from Neo-Idealism,[167] from Protestant premises,[168] from those who demand a social order based on respect for the dignity of the human person,[169] and from those who are trying to reduce values to those sociological conditions which —in view of the pretended relativity of all values—had remained as the only absolute, with the result that valuations were regarded as a basic function of human coexistence.[170]

We are able to see now that the different scales of values are in direct proportion to the different ways in which the nature of man is metaphysically defined. A cursory survey of some of the most significant attempts of contemporary European philosophy shows the need to free the discussion of values from the limitations of theoretical speculation and to subordinate it to the question concerning the fate of the West and the "Western crisis." It is quite evident, however, that *the answers given merely restate positions which were already taken in the course of the nineteenth century and that the problems under discussion have remained unresolved to this day. The interrelation of these problems with those of technology and the technological interpretation of the world has* —with one notable exception—*not been recognized.*[171] But it is only when this interrelation is taken into account that the problems can be envisaged in a dimension where a solution may be found. In the following discussion we shall confine ourselves to the evolution that has occurred in German philosophy because it has been markedly successful in demonstrating this interrelation and in presenting certain perspectives which seem to make it possible to untangle the confusion so prevalent in the more conventional inquiry into the nature of those values and norms which are to guide human action.

If, however, we want to understand this evolution of thinking, we must first of all take a look at *the situation from which it started:* we must clearly envisage the way in which the attempt to arrive at specific norms of action and the conception of the nature of man are interconnected. This original situation was in very large measure determined by the anthropological turn which German thought had taken since the breakdown of German Idealism. Man had become fully conscious of the great power which the tools of modern science had given into his hands. While at the beginning of modern times the definition of man as *animal rationale* was still generally accepted, his *ratio,* deployed in science, was now understood as the power of gaining mastery of the world. The course of the evolution of the modern mind was thus interpreted as involving *the self-realization of man by virtue of the power of his scientific reasoning.* This means that man now recognized himself as a being who in his freedom is capable of making himself "to be what he is," and who, by virtue of his freedom, impresses his stamp upon the world by means of dominating it technologically. It was in this sense that *Karl Marx* could demand that man must comprehend himself as a being or essence which has the power of "making itself." It goes without saying that in this context human thoughts are not "past" but ever "present" and ever efficacious. Simultaneously, for Marx the philosophic-intellective interpretation of the world has been reduced to an ideological superstructure, to something which is actually determined by and depending on the dialectical necessities of a communal life which fabricates itself. To the extent that the existing social conditions are accepted as simply "given," man is already alienated from his essence, for he is no longer aware of the fact that these conditions are of his own making. He achieves his "theoretical liberation" when he becomes aware of this, and the consequence of this liberation is man's transition to that practical "real liberation" which is consummated in social revolution. This revolution is, however, not in the true sense an act of man but rather the realization of a dialectical necessity which as such determines the point at which man's self-alienation—

which had reached its peak in the self-alienated proletariat—turns into its opposite, namely, the return of man to his own true essence. The preceding theoretical liberation—in the form of a critique of those ideological superstructures that transfigure the "given" world, such as religions and philosophic systems—and the sociological derivation of all ruling norms and values from particular historical-social conditions, is not intended to be a relativistically oriented survey but denotes *the return to the truth of reality,* a return to the productive-creative process of the "self-made" human community. The *process of historical evolution, too, is understood by Marx as a process of labor, a process of "making."* In the place of the *animal rationale* steps thus *homo faber* (i.e., man the "maker," man the fabricator) who, as a laboring member of the community integrates himself in the general process of production. *The fully accomplished liberation of man signalizes therefore simultaneously his self-surrender as a self-made personality.* This latter ideal is unmasked as a bourgeois ideology. We see then that the fully accomplished liberation of man means within the Marxist frame of reference *a liberation from human individuality.* In other words, man has returned from self-alienation to his own nature when, as an individual, he becomes one with the "essence of the species." "Socialized man" thus represents for Marx the truth of the human nature or essence.

While the initial situation—which is centered in the problem of the interrelation of knowledge and action—is generally characterized by the modern emancipation of man, the basic idea of Karl Marx shows that *there exists a necessary interconnection between the liberation of man for the tasks of technical-scientific world domination and man's total integration in the universal process of labor. It therefore seems to be essentially impossible to affirm or approve positively the movement toward emancipation and at the same time to deny or to negate the Marxist conclusions.*

The inner connection of these consequences with the entire history of ideas in the Western world as well as the internal logic with which these consequences follow from the basic ideas which have been alive since the beginnings of the modern age, became clearly visible only in our own time. It became evident that it is impossible to explain Marxism philosophically as resulting from a mere misunderstanding of Hegel's thinking but that Marx simply saw the consequences of the inherent tendencies of the modern age more clearly and developed the conclusions more radically than anyone else. In the evolution of thought in the nineteenth century Marx plays a much more essential part than those eclectic thinkers and systems which filled the tomes dedicated to the history of philosophy in the nineteenth century. In most of these works Marx is disposed of with only a brief passing reference. The recognition of Marx's real significance is conducive, however, to a new understanding of the continuity of an evolution which already harbors those contrasts and conflicts which agitate our present day world.[172] Only now does it become possible to envisage the point of view from which these conflicts can be met head-on, with some prospect of redetermining the interrelationship of knowledge and action. Here too therefore the historical clarification of the origins of our present situation is an unconditional presupposition for an understanding of the tasks deriving from this situation. And we shall now have to trace the most important steps that were taken in this direction.

Our inquiry must first of all take account of *Max Scheler's* "sociology of knowledge"(*Wissenssoziologie*).[173] As far as its origins are concerned, the program of this type of sociology can be traced back to the social doctrine of Karl Marx. Once it was freed from the dogmatic one-sidedness of its "ideology," [174] Marx's doctrine of society led to a deeper understanding of the interrelation of social and economic conditions and of the philosophico-religious premises of certain economic systems, on the one hand,[175] and the sociological factors underlying specific ideals of science and knowledge, on the other. In this context, Scheler developed his doctrine of the interrelation of real and ideal factors,[176] designating "blood," "power," and "economics" as the three main groups of "real" factors. In addition, we find in his work already some hints (in the form of *aperçus,* without detailed historical documentation) that point to the connections between the Christian-spiritualistic idea of God and that de-spiritualization of nature which prepared the way for modern natural science.[177] He attempts to show that *any kind of cognitive seizure of existing entities presupposes a correlative axiological experience.* He tried to substantiate this doctrine in his theory of emotional experiences—in which all valuations are said to originate—and in his doctrine of the hierarchy of values, which avers that the values correspond to the different levels or spheres of human nature—the "vital," the psychical, and the spiritual sphere.

It was *Franz Brentano* who first pointed to emotional experiences as the source of the evidence contained in axiological consciousness [178]—an idea which was adopted by Husserl and developed by him into the doctrine of the "right" that is imparted to man by every kind of perception—sensory, psychical, and spiritual. These suggestions as well as the acceptance of Pascal's idea of the *ordre du coeur* as against the order of rational knowledge provided the basis of Scheler's doctrine of axiological experiences and axiological evidence. In a similar vein *Nicolai Hartmann* developed his axiology as a doctrine of "ideal being," to which corresponds the direct seizure in acts of valuation, acts which have their roots in those emotional acts which represent the aboriginal "feeling for values" (*Wertgefühl*).[179]

The horizon of all these axiological doctrines is limited by the fact that they are trying to relate "values" to the timelessly constant structure of human nature. Only Scheler's "sociology of knowledge" is free from this limtiation in that he attempts to use the insight into the emotional-experiential origins of axiological evidence for finding an answer to the question concerning the origins of the modern concept of science and to trace modern science back to the structure of the drives *(Triebstruktur)* underlying the modern bourgeois concept of man. The supposed "freedom from value judgments" in the search for that which "exists objectively" is thus unmasked as *an idea which is itself conditioned by a value judgment.* It is conditioned "by the 'vital' value which is embodied in a world view—a world view which comprises exclusively those elements of natural phenomena which are important for world domination." [180] Technology and science put this neatly together "since they represent parallel consequences of one and the same psychoenergetic process." [181] "The formal-mechanical schema of nature which makes possible its domination by technology and science is thus not a product of mere theory but rather the product of pure logic and mathematics and of the pure application of the value of power in the selection of that which can be observed in nature." [182] The contemplative mentality of the Middle Ages did not submit and succumb to this ardent desire for scientific-technical world domination and was therefore regarded by the modern age as "sterile." This negative judgment sealed, in Scheler's opinion, the defeat of the medieval *Weltanschauung.* From the specific premises of his axiology Scheler thus calls attention to *the historical interconnection between the problem of knowledge and the problem of labor.* It is in this context that the aforementioned position of Marx in its inherent possibilities and necessities becomes understandable. This understanding in turn casts light also on the role which science plays within the frame of Bolshevism, and explains why the latter can tolerate only one particular brand of "science."

Scheler does not confine himself, however, to examining these historical constellations—which make it clear that the modern concept of knowledge is inseparably linked with the goal of technological world domination—but he tries to answer the question as to the manner in which the meaning of knowledge must be re-interpreted if an escape from this fateful circle is to be found. He arrived at the conviction that the absolutization of mechanical reality which within the frame of historical materialism had led to the doctrine of "ideologies," was not at all based on a striving for "knowledge without any presuppositions" but rather rested on a philosophico-metaphysical foundation, namely, on the ideology of the rising modern bourgeois society.[183] He concluded from this that the sequel of this development—the dual phenomenon of Nihilism and technological world domination—could be overcome only if and when an ancient concept of knowledge was reinstated: knowledge must once again be understood as participation of one entity in the pure essential being *(Sosein)* of another entity, as a relationship which does neither co-posit nor aim at any transformation of the cognized being. The cognitive attitude must thus—in contrast to the attitude of modern science—be *non-aggressive;* it must be an attitude of "giving" and of "receptivity." The ultimate root of such a self-transcending participation in the pure essence of being may be formally characterized as "love." [184]

Heidegger has repeatedly referred to the intellectual stimuli which he received from Scheler's ideas, and there is hardly any doubt that those analyses of Heidegger which deal with the problem of the technical-scientific "will to power" that characterizes the modern age owe much to Scheler's influence, even though it is equally certain that Heidegger adds a new depth dimension to Scheler's historical and systematic horizon. Scheler discusses the pre-conditions of the development which led to the nihilistic impasse of the technological understanding of the world and which were thus responsible for the modern "crisis," from a purely sociological point of view, and he confines his discussion to the beginnings of the modern age. One of Heidegger's basic themes, on the other hand, is *the continuity that exists between the spirit of the modern age* and that of the preceding centuries and, quite generally, *the entire metaphysical structure of Western thinking.* It is the ultimate aim of his inquiry to understand the technological world view and the Nihilism of the present age as the consistent and necessary conclusion and culmination of Western metaphysics rather than as a mere accidental mishap.

The following, in short, is, according to Heidegger, the end result of the course of Western metaphysics: Already in

Plato's attempt to relate existing entities to the World of Ideas—an attempt which marks the beginnings of Western metaphysics—Heidegger discerns a preliminary form of the turn toward the conviction that "knowledge is power" (Francis Bacon), a conviction which in its articulated form signalizes the beginnings of modern times. The entire Western metaphysics, he argues, is in its basic tendency "humanistic" in this sense. "I am using this word here in its essential meaning and therefore in the broadest sense. According to this view, 'humanism' denotes an event which is inseparably linked with the beginning, the unfolding, and the end of metaphysics—the event which pushes man, in several directions but always in his essential being, into the center of all existing entities, but without making him the highest existing entity. 'Man' designates in this context 'manhood' or 'mankind,' either the individual or the community, either a people or a group of peoples. It is always a question of leading man, the *animal rationale* into the certitude of his destination and into the security of his 'life.' And this is to be accomplished within the realm of a firmly jointed basic metaphysical structure, so that his potentialities may be liberated and actualized. And this is being done for the sake of impressing upon man the stamp of his 'moral' behavior, for the sake of the salvation of his immortal soul, for the sake of the deployment of his creative powers, the formative development of his reason, the cultivation of his communal feelings, the disciplining of his body, or any suitable coupling of any or all of these 'humanisms.' In each of these instances everything—within a more or less narrow or more or less broad circumference—revolves around man, and the manner of the revolving is always metaphysically determined. Simultaneously with the culmination of metaphysics, humanism too presses on to the most extreme, that is, the most unconditional 'positions.' "[185]

According to this interpretation, metaphysics is a process in which man knowingly takes hold of his nature or essence *(Wesen)*. He gains mastery over his own self and his potentialities in the most diverse directions. And the beginnings of this development are to be found in Plato's doctrine of Ideas. For when all understanding of existing entities is traced back to a visualization of the realm of Eternal Ideas, then man, by virtue of his being able to visualize Ideas intellectually, is capable of comprehending his faculty of knowledge as an instrument of his power. As the possessor of such a knowledge of Ideas he is capable of projecting his world in advance and of projecting and designing an image of his self. History in its factual course and the experiences relating to it, cannot contribute anything essentially new, that is, nothing that was not already encompassed by man's projecting *a priori* thinking. Man is therefore believed to be capable of anticipating the future in his planning. But it is only in modern science that this capacity of thinking Ideas *(Ideendenken)* has revealed itself in its extreme possibilities as a tool of the human "will to power." For if the being of all things—their truth—is seen as something over which man, by virtue of his capacity of thinking Ideas, can gain mastery—rather than as something that in its facticity must be *given* to him again and again—then the road is open that leads to the conviction that all the truths of human knowledge are merely and exclusively "posited" by man, are merely subjective valuations which he needs for the actualization of his will power.

This final conclusion Heidegger discerns in *Nietzsche's doctrine of "the Will to Power,"* which he regards as *the last word of Western metaphysics*—a conclusion, however, which was already implicit at the very beginning. After the legend of Nietzsche's plan for his *opus magnum* (i.e. *The Will to Power*) has been destroyed, we may well doubt whether Nietzsche himself regarded this doctrine as his "last word." [186] However, Heidegger's interpretation is thereby by no means invalidated, since it makes no claim to encompass Nietzsche's work as a whole. "We never understand," Heidegger writes, "on the basis of a popular idea of will and power, what 'Will to Power' in Nietzsche's sense really means. We can learn to understand this meaning only by way of reflecting on the nature of metaphysical thinking, that is, by reflecting on the meaning of the entire history of Western metaphysics." [187] For if all the truths that can be known are "posited" by life itself—a life which in its essence is a positing of values *(Wertschätzung)*—then all knowledge is only the means by which life gains mastery over existing entities. These entities are then nothing in themselves, and every truth is only a product of the volitional movement of life. And what is the object of life's volition? Life desires its self-preservation and self-elevation, and—to achieve its self-elevation—it produces the norms of its actions. Nietzsche's "devaluation of all values" and his unmasking of truth as illusion imply the demand not to be bound by any already "given" value but to recognize as the highest value Life itself—a life which posits values and which in its progressive movement destroys systems of values —and to learn to understand life's will to self-preservation and self-elevation. Every truth is therefore to be measured by the services it renders to life. *Truth* accordingly is "a condition posited by the Will to Power, the pre-condition of the preservation of power, and as such truth is a value." [188] *Nihilism* with its insight that "there is nothing behind any supposed permanence"—that the permanence which we believe we seize in knowledge is nothing but an illusion without any foundation in reality except Life itself with its Will to Power —is a necessary consequence of man's confidence in the power of his knowledge of ideas and values, which, it seems to him, makes him capable of embracing knowingly the totality of all existing entities *(das Ganze des Seienden).* Nihilism is a *necessary* consequence which must become manifest precisely because the belief in the *power* of this kind of knowledge is illusory. And it is Life itself which creates this illusion. If Heidegger's view is correct, then *the technological Will to Power and Nihilism,* understood as the waylessness of the "whereto" or "whither" of this human possibility of domination, *must have its roots already in the original metaphysical disposition of the Western mind.*

By pointing out these interdependent developments a key may have been found that will enable us to grope our way through the confusing maze of our present situation and through the disparate attempts at discovering a new axiological foundation that may make it possible to overcome Nihilism. For the confusion derives from the fact that the desperate desire to oppose to the negation of personal human freedom—consummated in Marxism in a paradoxical reversal of Marx's original position—a counter-thesis, has actually been unsuccessful in getting rid of the premises which underly the conclusions of Marxism. The thinking in terms of "values" and "ideas" grows, after all, out of the same basic drive for man's absolute autonomy—an autonomy based on the faculty of knowledge—that is also the root of Marxism. A reawakened consciousness of the original sources of axiological evidence—hidden in the subject—is therefore not enough. For the dichotomy which implies a split between a subject harboring axiological inner experiences and an objectively existing, theoretically knowable "external" world—a dichotomy which has led to the estrangement of "science" and *"Weltanschauung"*—is a result of the same development.

To overcome these opposites and to call a halt to the domineering rule of a technological understanding of the world and the ensuing nihilistic "crisis," it is not sufficient to resurrect one of the traditional forms of axiology, whether it be the ancient concept of knowledge—as an apperception of entities in the light of Ideas—or the neo-humanistic ideals which are inseparable from the problems of human freedom, or the revived acknowledgment of the Christian cosmos of values. For it is a mistake to assume that the past history of the Western mind comprises a stock of absolutely indubitable truths which can simply be revived. The ultimate conquest of Nihilism can be prepared only by a kind of thinking that leaves altogether behind the "humanism" of Western thought. For, as Heidegger phrases it, this kind of humanism "underestimates the dignity of human nature" because it defines this nature as "fixed" *(feststehend)* once and for all and thus implies "a fixed interpretation of nature, of history, of the world, of the world-ground, that is, of the totality of all that which is *(des*

Seienden im Ganzen)."[189] The *"con-versio" (die Kehre)* which is demanded of Western thought, requires that *man learns to recognize the limits of his claim to a seizure of "the totality of all that which is" by means of his knowledge, since this claim leads inevitably to the subordination of knowledge to volition (Wille).* This false claim must be opposed by the acknowledgment that man is not able to seize his own nature by means of an intuitive vision of the "Idea" (*Ideenblick*) but —"ex-sisting," that is, standing-out into the realm of Being —must *experience* and *re-experience* his nature in ever new and different situations, as that which is "measured" or "meted out" to him by the history of Being.[190] *The possibility of any knowledge* a priori *thus rests on a much deeper ground: it rests on the experience of Being in its historicity.* What is required, therefore, is not a new definition of the nature or essence of man but a new attitude with respect to existing entities, an attitude which "lets entities be" whatever and in whatever they are, an attitude which sees in things no longer objects which can be manipulated and dominated at will but which asks first what a thing is. Such an attitude is willing to be recruited in the service of Being instead of desiring to press Being into the service of a knowledge which is directed by the will.

To regain a unification of knowledge and action it is therefore not enough to demonstrate the emotional basis of all knowledge and to show that there is no such thing as a "science without presuppositions" nor its correlate, an "objective world." This does not mean that those investigations which are trying to disclose the historical and sociological foundations of specific ideals of knowledge and life and the foundations of those "values" which provide guidance for living, are useless. They have indeed led to a deeper insight into the structural laws of human-historical coexistence, insights which have been reaching greater depths than those of Pragmatism and the historical views of Enlightenment, and greater depths than Hegel's dialectical schema and its reversal and dogmatic hardening in Marxism. They have, however, not been able to inquire successfully into the ultimate reasons and causes that underly this historical becoming, chiefly because they all have started out from the presupposition that this historical evolution could be grasped and expressed in a *concept,* whether it be the notion of divine Providence or of the Absolute Spirit or of the conditions of production or of the Will to Power. A metaphysical answer of this kind underlies implicitly also the above mentioned attempt to answer the question as to the origin of values, and the answer is a metaphysical one even when the inquirers believe that they are proceeding in a strictly empirical manner. For the conviction that it is possible to establish the origin of values in a strictly empirico-sociological manner, implies a presupposition with regard to a structure of the universe that is easily accessible to the grasp of knowledge. This is once again a metaphysical presupposition and of such a compelling nature that its consequences are inescapable.

We see then that an attitude which implants in man the conviction that existing entities can be manipulated and dominated at will, can never lead to the overcoming of Nihilism and is unable to make man capable of imparting a new meaning to the apparatus of technology which he administers. This can be accomplished only by an attitude which renounces this false claim and which thereby also renounces a "humanism" in the previously discussed sense, that is, a humanism which in its thinking is totally man-centered and is obsessed with the will to a self-centered self-possession. It is therefore not the task of philosophic thinking to plan and organize this *con-versio,* for all that philosophic thinking is called to do is, in "thinking of Being" (*Andenken an das Sein*), to remember what is necessary if a new "mittence" is to become manifest for man.[191]

The writings of *Ortega y Gasset* point in a similar direction without, however, drawing the same far reaching conclusions regarding the overcoming of Western metaphysics and its particular kind of "humanism." Ortega's inquiries revolve around the historical premises of the crisis of modern man.

In one of his early works he viewed this crisis in one of its main aspects, the "Revolt of the Masses." In his later writings [192] he appropriated some of the ideas of Dilthey and of the representatives of Phenomenology. They aided him in his attempt *to understand* the crisis of modern man as a crisis of modern man's basic philosophic position. This in turn led him to a further search for the roots of the technological world view and to a clearer visualization of the problem of the possibilities to transcend this point of view. He was convinced that the world-problem of technology cannot be mastered and resolved if it is simply regarded as a technical problem, since the project of the transformation of a "life-program" has its locus in a deeper layer of civilization than the layer in which the plans and designs of world-organization are localized. The modern crisis—which Ortega understands as a "crisis of reason" in Nietzsche's sense—can, in his opinion, be resolved only by a "new revelation." He does not mean to suggest—as has sometimes been wrongly assumed—that Christian revelation must be superseded by a new "Advent" but rather that this new "revelation" is already implicit in the visualization of the historicity of human *Dasein.* Once this idea is taken seriously, man can open himself anew for the message of Christian revelation.[193]

One of the consequences of the required turn-about in man's attitude is that the *concept of labor* gains a new meaning and significance: human nature can no longer be measured by the amount of labor which the individual performs. The goal of giving back to man his dignity can be reached only by transcending the narrow frame of the "humanism" of Western metaphysics and by overcoming the present generally prevalent idolization of labor and performance. This problem has been thoroughly discussed by *Joseph Pieper* in a dialogue with *Ernst Jünger*. The latter, in an earlier period of his life and work, had tried to use the figure of the "workingman" to advance a very positive interpretation of Nihilism.[194] Pieper, conversely, is trying to show that only the overcoming of the ideology of a totalitarian world of labor can restore to human life the blessings of leisure and festive cultic celebration. "The justification of leisure is not that the functionary should function with as little disturbing interruption as possible but that the functionary should find it possible to remain a human being, that he be not wholly absorbed by the constricted *milieu* of his limited function, that he should remain capable of seeing the world as a whole and thus to fulfill himself and to come face to face with that totality of Being to which his own personal being is ordained." To attain to this, however, "humanism" and the frame of reference of the *humanum* are insufficient. For "the quintessence of leisure is that festive celebration from which derive the possibility as well as the legitimacy of leisure. . . . This celebration, however, is religious and cultic in its nature.[195] There is no genuine festive celebration without the gods, and the meaning of this kind of celebration is enthusiastic rapture *(das Entrücktwerden).*"

These words make it evident that the victory over Nihilism and over the totalitarian laboring-world of technology can come to us only from the realm of religion, from the realm of "the holy," to use Heidegger's term. And this insight leads us to the final question we intend to discuss, the question of the interrelation of philosophy and religion, of knowledge and faith.

CHAPTER VII

The Problem of Being: Philosophy and Theology

The preceding sketchy outlines have shown that contemporary European philosophy in all its branches seeks to transcend the thematic anthropological foundation from which it started and that in this attempt it breaks through the narrow framework of the traditional division of its problems in several separate disciplines. Before concluding our inquiry, we must now ask how contemporary European philosophy pictures the object of this transcendence and how it views its own nature, or how and where it draws the lines that separate it from science, art, and religion. For the nature of philosophy can be understood only from the perspective of its highest intentional object. Let us ask therefore: what is this highest intentional object of contemporary philosophy, the object which aids in its self-understanding and which justifies us in interpreting its basic tendency as the will to transcend the problems of anthropology?

We have made frequent references to "Being," and the inquiry into the nature of Being is indeed the fundamental quest of philosophy. The answers given to this question constitute in their sequence the history of metaphysics. But does the transcending of the problems of anthropology that is characteristic of contemporary European philosophy simply mean a "resurrection of metaphysics" in the sense of a return to this ancient fundamental question or does this transcending signalize a breaking through the horizon of traditional metaphysics?

As a matter of fact, both of these things have been happening in contemporary European philosophy. But we may well ask whether both of these tendencies are equally significant or whether it can be shown that the attempt to transcend the total horizon of Western metaphysics is, philosophically speaking, far more significant than all the efforts that have been made to bring about a renewal of metaphysics without breaking through the frame of the traditional basic philosophic questions. What does it really mean to transcend the horizon of Western metaphysics?

It would seem that it is permissible to speak of this kind of transcendence only if it can be shown that the traditional problems of metaphysics are rather narrowly limited and that this limitation can and must be done away with. Heidegger called this limitation of Western metaphysics its "forgetfulness of Being." [196] But in what sense can the history of Western metaphysics be understood as the history of the "forgetfulness" or "forgottenness" of Being if the question as to the nature of Being has been the warp and woof of the entire history of metaphysics?

Within what frame of reference, then, can the *concept of Being* be determined in contemporary European philosophy? In order to understand to what extent the currently attempted determinations lie within the confines of the metaphysical tradition and to what extent they transcend these confines, it is first of all necessary to characterize briefly this frame. We find that it is determined by the opposites of being and becoming, truth and appearance, essence *(Wesen)* and factual ontic existence *(Tatsache)* as well as by the manner in which these opposites are determined in their mutual relationship and by the way in which they explicitate or illumine each other. From the very beginnings of Western metaphysics there is never any doubt that Being is *constant* and *permanent* as against the world of becoming. That which is permanent is regarded as *true,* and its truth is discovered in speech, in so far as speech is predicative; and the modes of predications—the categories—are the modes in which Being is enunciated and by means of which a greater or lesser amount of Being is distinguished in that which is *(im Seienden).* But even that which —as changeable being—ranks lower in the scale of Being, can be verified as such, as "this-there," as this determined entity that offers itself to sensory experience, if it is related to what is Being and constancy in it, namely, its permanent nature or essence. Being is thus interpreted as essence *(essentia* —literally: "beingness" [*die Seiendheit*]*).* The essence is that which makes a thing what it is, which "lets it be" as that which it is. And this essence is distinguished from the fact *that* it is—its *Dasein*—the fact that an entity of this essence is actualized existentially here and now. And since the essence is that which alone makes it possible to predicate anything regarding that which factually exists—so that a reference to the essence is necessarily presupposed in any predication concerning a factually existing entity—the essence is *the necessary* as against the contingency that attaches to any factual realization of an individual of this general essence.

The factual realization depends on certain conditions. The fact that an individual existent of an essence is actualized, that, for example, a human being—that is, an individual existent of the essence "man"—is born and that thus the potentiality inherent in the essence "man" is actualized, depends on certain causes, and the question concerning the actualization of essences leads to the question concerning a *first cause.* This latter cannot itself be again mere potentiality but must rather be pure actuality. And since within the frame of Christian throught the question concerning the first cause led to God as the Creator of all that which is, God was defined as pure actuality, as an Existent in whom essence and factual existence as individual entity of the essence cannot be separated: God's essence includes His existence. According to this premise, the essences of individual things are intelligible for man because they are foreknown [from eternity] in the divine Spirit. For they are in the divine Spirit as the prototypes *(Urbilder)* of all existing individual entities; the latter were created in the image of these eternal prototypes [i.e., the Ideas in the Divine Mind]. And since the human mind is a certain image and likeness of the Divine Mind, it can know *Truth as congruity of the Idea in the Divine Mind and its representation in the human mind.* For the Truth cognized by man rests on the *Aboriginal Truth,* that is, on the fact that all things are foreknown by God. In this sense, all things are true: *omne ens est verum.*

We do not intend to discuss here in detail how in the Western tradition of metaphysics Being has in different ways been defined as Truth, a Truth which makes possible the truth of knowledge. We should like to emphasize only the thoroughgoing basic fact that in the frame of the entire ancient as well as Christian tradition *essence precedes existence (Dasein). Etienne Gilson,* in his book entitled *"L'être et l'essence,"* has described the bifurcation in the concept of Being and existence as related to essence and has commented on the diverse possible positions which have been taken in the history of Western philosophy with respect to this interrelationship. He has shown that the motive force in this "being-existence-essence" relationship is always the dialectic tension between Being as essential permanence and factual existence, and that Being, understood as existence *(Dasein),* is the "rebellious element" [197] which metaphysics is trying again and again to eliminate. This shows in turn—though Gilson does not say so explicitly and does not draw any systematic conclusions from the fact—that traditional *Western philosophy is based on an ontology of essence.*

Catholic Neo-Thomism—represented today in many authentic works [198]—has clung to this ontology of essence and its anchorage of the intelligibility of essences and their hierarchy in the fore-knowing of God, the *actus purus.*

Although Kant, among others, undermined the presupposition of the possibility of man's metaphysical knowledge of

God and His attributes, the ontology of essence has never been radically called in question but has merely been given a different meaning: "The essence is that which is essential. To be essential, however, can now—since a glance into the nature of Being is no longer possible—mean only: to be essential for man, to be of indispensable significance for man, to be necessary for him. And the absolute essence is replaced by the relative essence, namely, the indispensable and necessary category of reason (*Verstand*), the indispensable and necessary idea of intellection *(Vernunft)*. But these essences are for man only auxiliary means of his being able to know and to act. Their validity does not lie in their envisaged normative absoluteness, as is the case with Plato's Ideas, nor in their relationship to Being, as is the case in the metaphysics of Thomas Aquinas, but solely in thier indispensability. It is therefore the meaning of a 'transcendental deduction' to offer a demonstration of this indispensability instead of an intuition of essences that is possible only for God." [199]

Neo-Thomism, in adhering to the traditional ontology as against the Kantian position, tried to justify its stand by the attempted demonstration that the metaphysics of *Wolff* and *Baumgarten*—with which Kant's negative critique was primarily concerned—rested largely on the preceding Protestant school-metaphysics (i.e., Protestant "scholasticism"), which had adopted the main theses of Thomistic ontology.[200] However, the Wolff-Baumgarten metaphysics had abandoned the all-important idea that the truth of all things rested in God. Consequently, the Neo-Thomists argued that Kant's critique was not aimed at all at Thomist metaphysics, since Kant's critique was dealing with an ontology that had been deprived of its very core.[201]

If the manner in which the interrelation of Being as essence and Being as *Dasein* (existence) is understood, determines the structure of philosophic systems, then the question must be raised whether the adherence to the precedence of essence versus *Dasein* remains possible within the frame of a world-interpretation that is based on the principle of having man occupy the place of God and of giving philosophy an anthropological foundation. When this happens, it appears that the idea of the Creator-God and therewith the relatedness of all things to their exemplary prototypes *(Urbilder)*—which is the very foundation of the Christian ontology of essences—is no longer self-evident. And it is in this situation that the revolt against this tradition—a revolt that is usually summarily referred to as "philosophy of existence"—has its origin. The common basic question which underlies the otherwise very divergent branches of this philosophic movement relates thus to that specific concept of truth which rests on the idea of all things being-foreknown in the Divine Mind. And it must be asked whether the corresponding determination of the interrelationship of essence and existence suffices to express philosophically the nature of man and his relationship to Being as well as to express the nature of Being itself. In other words, the adherence to a definition of the nature of man which asserts that the human essence precedes human existence as potentiality precedes actuality and which assumes that man's destiny is thus pre-determined, demands a "Ground of Being," namely, the all-knowing God, in whose fore-knowledge the potentialities of the particular essence are firmly pre-ordained.

It has always been one of the fundamental problems of theology to harmonize this fore-knowledge of God with human freedom, and this same problem reappears in the center of all the modern versions of this doctrine.[202] *Sartre,* too, in his essay titled "Existentialism Is a Humanism," points out that this idea of the constant-permanent nature or essence of man was adhered to in modern times even when its underlying reasons were no longer valid and the idea had thus become "ground-less." However, Sartre does not ask the important question why this "groundlessness" was not recognized. It is only *Heidegger* who, starting out in his investigations from the consequences of the historical consciousness,[203] has made these connections transparent. Man had to experience his own historicity before the conviction of a permanent-constant human nature could be shaken. Even though the idea of historicity itself could originally be conceived only within the frame of Christianity, it is quite evident that a serious consideration of this idea had to lead to an attack on the ontology of essences and that such an attack would open up entirely new possibilities for theology. "Serious consideration," however, meant in this instance nothing less than *the annulment of the forgottenness of Being.*

What then is the meaning of "forgottenness of Being" *(Seinsvergessenheit),* and how is it related to the prevalent rule of the ontology of essences? Forgottenness of Being means that the ambiguity inherent in the concepts of "existing" (*Seiend;* Gr., *on*) and of "Being" (*Sein;* Gr., *einai*) remained hidden to Western metaphysics from its very beginnings and that this concealedness has determined the fate of Western thought and the fate also of Christian theology. "Aristotle calls that science which views the existent *qua* existent *(das Seiende als das Seiende)* the 'First Philosophy.' The latter, however, does not only view the existent in its existing *(das Seiende in seiner Seiendheit)"*—pointing out the distinctions between the concept of essence and *Dasein* (existence)—"but it views simultaneously that Existent which represents existence in its purity, that is, the highest Existent. This highest Existent (Gr., *to theion*), the Divine, is referred to with a strange ambiguity as 'Being' *(das Sein).* The 'First Philosophy' is—as ontology—also a theology of that which truly 'is' *(das Seiende).* It would be more correct to call the First Philosophy a 'theiology.' The science of 'that which is' as such *(des Seienden als solchen)* is onto-theological." [204] The strange ambiguity to which Heidegger refers here lies in the fact that all the questions concerning the modes of existing and concerning that Existent which ranks highest, are already imbued with the light of the meaning which the words "is" and "being" have and that, on the other hand, *this Light itself does not become the object of the questioning, because the questioning is concerned only with that which "appears" in this Light.* In order to speak meaningfully of something and to predicate of something that "it is," one must first understand the meaning of *Being.* In other words, the astounding fact that there "is" anything at all and not rather nothing at all, must already have been accepted as a matter of course. However, in this acceptance that which is supposedly already understood and taken for granted, is completely forgotten, and the only thing that is kept in view is that which within the horizon of this "already-understood" appears as "existing." The inquiry is thus exclusively concerned with the existential mode of a particular being's entity. If simultaneously an ambiguous reference is made to "Being," it becomes evident that Being itself has fallen into oblivion. For "Being" is not that which has a maximum of existence *(das am meisten Seiende)* but rather that in the light of which—and man is the "there-being" *(Da-Sein)* of this light—the question concerning a hierarchical order of existing entities can be meaningfully asked and God can be defined as the highest Existent. In any number of variations God is understood as "substance," and substance is that which makes every existing entity what it is, whether substance is defined as intellect or will or spirit or reason, or as pure actuality, an actuality which no longer contains any admixture of non-actualized potentiality. Substance thus means essence *(Wesen),* that is, the existing of the existent (*die Seiendheit des Seienden*). The question, however, as to what makes existents intelligible in their existence is simply not being asked. This makes it quite manifest that "Christian theology in its knowledge and in the mode and manner of its knowledge is metaphysics." [205]

That Christian theology is metaphysics accounts also for that "humanism" which underlies Western thought,[206] a humanism which has not only a too low estimation of man but also of God. All its determinations of "Being" and of God—as "Supreme Being"—have grown out of the human efforts to understand existing entities in their existence, their modes and their hierarchical order. And this kind of "existing" is ambiguously referred to as "Being." All these determinations, however, presuppose a "ground" which is hidden from man.

This presupposition entails the fact that "Being" has become "illumined" *(gelichtet),* so that in the sheen of this illumination every entity can manifest itself in its "existing," and God can reveal Himself in His Selfhood. Metaphysics, on the other hand, "thinks the existent *qua* existent. Whenever the question as to the quiddity of existents is being asked, only existing entities as such come into view. Metaphysical thinking owes this kind of view to the light of Being. This light—that is, the light experienced by this kind of thinking—is not itself envisaged, since the metaphysical view sees existing entities only *qua* existing entities. From this point of view metaphysical thinking, to be sure, asks the question as to the 'existing source' and as to the author of the light. This light itself is believed to be sufficiently luminous, owing to the fact that it allows to every view a clear vision of existing entities." [207]

As against these shortcomings of metaphysical thinking, it is the task and function of "foundational thinking" *(wesentliches Denken)* to revert to the "hidden ground" of metaphysics. "Foundational" thinking "thinks of the Truth of Being as such." [208] Metaphysics, on the other hand, "is excluded from the experience of Being by its very nature" because it pays no heed to the ambiguity of "being" and "existing," that is, it "pays never any heed to what is concealed in the very unconcealedness of this *on.*" [209] "Foundational thinking," going back in its questioning to this concealed ground, is therefore "the foundation of ontology." Its first step is the analysis of human *Dasein,* and this analysis—as a fundamental ontology—transcends traditional ontology in every respect.[210] The fact that this analysis encounters on its way "the fundamental state-of-mind of dread" *(die Grundbefindlichkeit der Angst)* as a dread of nothingness, means that it has entered the dimension of foundational thinking—that is, "the remembrance of Being" *(An-denken an das Sein).* For viewed from the standpoint of existing entities, "Being" appears as "nothing." That which "lets be" all existing entities in their existence and their essence, cannot itself be an existing entity, and because it cannot be understood in this sense, it was forgotten in the metaphysical inquiry into the *on*. From this point of view Heidegger understands Nihilism as the necessary end-phase of Western metaphysics, as an end which, however, is already implicit in its beginning, an end that carries with it the insight which remained hidden for metaphysics, namely, "Being is steeped in the 'not' of negativity," (*dass es mit dem Sein nichts ist*).[211] This insight, however, must not be regarded as signalizing the shipwreck of all the efforts of thinking but—if Nihilism is to be overcome—as a demand for foundational thinking, as a demand for "the return to the ground of metaphysics." This does of course not mean that all that is required is a new exertion of thought. What foundational thinking has to tell mankind in the future cannot be outlined in the form of a program or a system of a future "philosophy of man." It is rather a question of the "mittence" *(Schickung)* of Being, as was also the limitation of thinking in the form of the "forgottenness of Being." This "mittence grows out of the situation in which the nature of Western man had its habitat. The confusion can therefore not be disentangled by merely redefining the words *on* and *einai,* so as to determine more exactly the meaning of 'existing' *(seiend)* and 'being' *(sein).* The attempt, on the other hand, to pay incessantly heed to the confusion and to break eventually its stubborn force, might some day provide the occasion for a different re-solution of the 'mittence' of Being." [212] The task of contemporary European philosophy can therefore be no more and no less than to do this preparatory work.

As we have pointed out before, this reference to the "mittence Being" must be taken as a strong hint that the ultimate that be-falls *(zu-fällt)* man and that makes it possible for him to gain the horizon of all his certitudes and all his knowledge is not the product of his own activity and effort but is to be accepted by him as a free gift. However, Heidegger does not engage here in speculations on the interrelation of freedom and grace, for such speculations would already presuppose the intelligibility of this mysterious interrelationship.

As a matter of fact, the problem of the incomparable uniqueness and ineffableness of the "ground of Being"—as against all the predicable relationships that prevail in the realm of existing entities—makes its appearance at diverse junctures in the history of Western thought. This should perhaps caution us not to generalize the dictum of the "forgottenness of Being" in Western metaphysics. This reproach applies above all to a predominant basic feature in an historical trend that has its culminating point in Hegel's logic. This philosophic trend is characterized by the attempt to bring the interrelationship of "existents" *(Seiendes)* and "being" into the grip of speculative knowledge.

What tends to mislead and confuse us in the present situation is the fact that most of the thinkers who have adopted decisive ingredients of Heidegger's thinking—so that it has become customary to apply to all these philosophic developments the summary titles "philosophy of existence" or "existentialism"—have not followed Heidegger on his way to the "thinking of Being" and in his "return to the ground of metaphysics." This is in particular true of *Sartre,* whose "revolt against a metaphysics of essences remains within the traditional schema of this very same metaphysics; he merely attempts to reverse the position, the weight and the significance of the poles of this traditional schema of *essentia* and *existentia.* This means that he tries to revolutionize this kind of metaphysics by putting its basic concepts upside-down." Sartre's existentialism is thus an attempt "to uproot the metaphysical construct of scholasticism on its own ground." This kind of existentialism is *"a metaphysics of essences with a negative (minus) sign* and becomes intelligible only from the point of view and within the frame of essentialism." [213] While Sartre's metaphysics is anti-theological in that it proclaims the total emancipation of the absolutely free and autonomous human being, it fulfills nonetheless a positive function by developing in its penetrating analyses a sort of philosophy of privation which points to a place of emptiness or vacancy in human consciousness without, however, being able to fill this void, owing to the limitations imposed by Sartre's own premises.

Christian existentialism, too, seems to remain within the horizon of Western metaphysics. True enough—as against Aristotelian-Thomistic philosophy which grounds the truth of things in their being-known by God—it reverts to scholastic *voluntarism* and tries to relate human *Dasein* in its concretely apperceived individual existence to the *Pure Act* by understanding Being as active actuality. While in Christian existentialism man is thus no longer placed inside the frame of a fixed metaphysics of order, the equation of God as *actus purus* and Being remains without doubt within the horizon of Western metaphysics.[214] Heidegger's inquiry into Being, on the other hand, *transcends this alternative of either intellectualism or voluntarism.* This alternative is meaningful only on the basis of traditional Western metaphysics because it interprets the essence of God by means of concepts, concepts which are being transferred from or projected by personal human experience.

The philosophy of existence of *Karl Jaspers*—by opposing the realm of the knowable to a Transcendence which can be experienced only in a presentiment gained by the shipwreck of knowledge that occurs in the human limit-situations—remains likewise within the frame of the antitheses of Western metaphysics. For on one side he places the realm of the objectively knowable—with the implicit absolutization of the objectivistic concept of knowledge that is a characteristic of modern philosophy—while on the other side stands the realm of a "philosophic faith" that is founded on the overtness of the individuated subject who realizes his existence, listening to the "ciphers" (i.e., the partially veiled symbolic language) of Transcendence. The human subject finds at his disposal the mythical images of the great world-religions, in which he may discern something "eternally true" that cannot be articulated in language but only hopefully surmised.[215] Such a philosophic religion leaves no room for a theology which interprets that certitude of faith upon which in a factual-historical sense every epoch rests. For such a theology is based on the presupposition that it is possible for human *Dasein* to rise above the facticity of a particular historical situation and its specific horizons to a supra-temporal anticipatory presentiment of some—quite undetermined and undefined—"transcendent" divine reality.[216] It need hardly be emphasized that this doctrine of something "eternally true" is closely linked with a fundamental schema of Western metaphysical thought and implies a purely subjectivistic interpretation of the dimension of religion. It can certainly not do justice to the reality of a religious faith which—as the factual-historical foundation of the communal existence of historical epochs—calls for simple acceptance. However, Jaspers himself is firmly convinced that the "scandal" of this kind of facticity can be circumvented by a certain mode of non-rationalistic but nonetheless "enlightened" thinking. Jaspers's construct of the "axial age" *(Achsenzeit)*—expounded in his philosophy of history[217]—shows clearly that the problem of the historicity of human *Dasein*—in the sense in which this problem has been elaborated in connection with the problem of *Dasein's* facticity—is foreign to his thinking.

For *Heidegger,* on the other hand, the way on which alone that dimension in which man can speak adequately of God, can come once again into view, is *a way of thinking*—a thinking which in a preparatory manner "holds open" the horizon within which something divine can reveal itself. If we ask further how he wants us to understand the relation of God to Being, he answers: Being in its clearing in human *Dasein* is the space in which God can reveal Himself. "The nature of the Holy can be thought only as deriving from the Truth of Being. And the nature or essence of the Godhead can be thought only as deriving from the nature of the Holy. What the word 'God' is to name can be thought and enunciated only in the light of the nature or essence of the Godhead. Is it not necessary, after all, to understand and listen to all these words with great care if as human beings—that is, as ex-sisting beings—we may be allowed to experience some kind of relatedness of God to man?" [218]

The answer to the question whether this relatedness is adequately experienced as a relatedness of Creator to creature and whether perhaps the clearing of Being, and *Dasein* as the clearing of Being, in its relationship to God can be thought in accordance with this schema,[219] must be left open until it has become clear whether this schema has any meaning at all —and, if so, what kind of meaning—outside the frame of metaphysical thinking. For in its traditional forms this schema is intimately linked with metaphysical thinking.

This being the case, what then is the mode and manner of "foundational thinking?" "Foundational thinking cannot begin until we have consciously experienced that the *ratio (Vernunft)* which has been glorified for many centuries is the most stubborn adversary of thinking." [220] "Foundational thinking" is *not conceptual thinking* in the sense of the traditional logic, according to which "the 'grasping' *(con-cipere)* in the manner of the representative 'con-cept' is regarded as the only possible way of getting hold of Being, a way or mode of seizure which is implied even where one has fled into the dialectic of concepts or into the non-conceptual realm of magical signs and symbols. It is forgotten altogether that the supremacy of the concept and the interpretation of thinking as 'seizure' rest already and exclusively on the un-thought—because un-experienced—natures of the *on* and the *einai*." [221] This does not mean that "foundational thinking" should be "illogical" and "irrational." It does mean that the *logos* of "foundational thinking" is still undeveloped and not understood. Such an understanding, however, presupposes a philosophic re-consideration of the nature of language and of the interrelationship that exists between the language of thought and the language of poetry. At any rate, the *logos* of hermeneutic (i.e., interpretative-descriptive) thinking will never have the meaning of a theoretical predication: it will have to find the fulfillment of its meaning not in theoretically cognitive experience but rather in the wholeness of a receptive attitude which encourages both theoretical acknowledgement and moral experience. It is in this sense that *Helmut Kuhn* has recently discussed the problem of the essential inseparability of the question of the nature of *Being* and the question of the nature of *Goodness* and has tried to demonstrate the ontology-producing nature of an experiential descent into the depth of conscience.[222]

The question might be asked whether "foundational thinking,"—once it surrenders the leading position of traditional logic—retains any guiding principle for its predications and whether this lack of a guiding principle does not prove the impossibility of referring back to that metaphysics which itself rests on the traditional logic. This question calls of necessity forth the counter-question: Can the thinking of the future stay within the boundaries of the traditional metaphysics once these boundaries have been sighted? For the fact that the boundaries have been sighted presupposes that a standpoint outside these boundaries has already been gained. The further fact that concerning this new standpoint and concerning that which can be seen from its perspective, nothing can yet be said that goes beyond certain limits, means simply that the inherent possibilities have not yet been actualized and that it will therefore be the function of the thinking of the future to finish this task.

Positivism cannot be overcome, and the idea of man's domination over his own self by means of a thinking that uses logic as its instrument *(organon)* cannot be abrogated by simply returning to a traditional metaphysics, whether it be the realistic *ordo-metaphysics* of Thomism or the metaphysics of Idealism. For all these positions have played their legitimate parts in the past, and they have neutralized one another in the struggle between different types of *Weltanschauung*. It all terminated in Positivism and Nihilism. And the metaphysics of the Will to Power—this most dangerous temptation of present-day man and the legitimate offspring of the entire evolution of Western thought—cannot be overcome by a mere *restoration* of whatever kind, that is, by a simple return to tradition. The metaphysics of the Will to Power can be overcome only when philosophic reflection is able to set the stage upon which the language of things and the call of God can again become audible, not only for the individual but for an entire historical community and society. The demand for "foundational thinking" does not call with the voice of prophesy for the advent of a new revelation. However, only when the requisites of foundational thinking are fulfilled can the revelation contained in the message of the Gospel become again audible in such a way that it can be understood by those in our day who listen to it. Such an understanding would not be possible, however, if this ancient revelation were again imprisoned in the forms of logico-ontological and metaphysico-theological thinking. For, imprisoned in this kind of thinking, this revelation has undergone disintegration in the course of an extended historical process, with the result that man has been split into a believing and a knowing being. For this reason the boundaries of metaphysical thinking and its concept of knowledge must be transcended if we want to learn anew what "faith" really is. Only when this happens will theology be in a position "to consider in deep seriousness the words of the Apostle and accordingly to consider in seriousness the 'foolishness' of philosophy." [223]

NOTES

1. G. W. F. Hegel, Preface to *Phänomenologie des Geistes* (2nd ed., Berlin, 1841). See bibliography for English translation.
2. Gaston Berger, *Philosophy and Phenomenological Research,* VII, 1 (1946), p. 10.
3. Cf. Ludwig Landgrebe, *Phänomenologie und Metaphysik,* Part III (Hamburg, 1949).
4. Cf. Max Scheler, *Deutsches Leben der Gegenwart* (Berlin, 1922).
5. Cf. Karl Löwith, *Von Hegel zu Nietzsche* (Zürich, 1941) (See bibliography for English translation) and Landgrebe, *Hegel und Marx. Marxismusstudien,* Vol. 1 (Tübingen, 1954), p. 39 sqq.
6. Cf. Martin Heidegger, *Holzwege* (Frankfurt a.M., 1950), esp. p. 98 sqq.
7. Cf. Martin Buber, *Das Problem des Menschen* (Heidelberg, 1948).
8. Cf. Heidegger, *loc. cit.*
9. Cf. José Ortega y Gasset, *Die Krise der Vernunft* (in *Europäische Revue,* XVIII, 3), p. 153.
10. Cf. Chap. VI of this volume.
11. Cf. Arnold Gehlen, *Der Mensch* (4th ed., Bonn, 1950).
12. Cf. Chap. IV of this volume.
13. A discussion of the problem of Nihilism will be found on pp. 148 sqq. and 158 sqq. of this volume.

14. Cf. Chap. IV of this volume.

15. Cf. Edmund Husserl, *Philosophie als strenge Wissenschaft* (in *Logos,* I, 1910); and *Husserliana* (The Hague: Martinus Nijhoff, 1950 sqq.). Cf. also *Ideen zu einer reinen Phänomenologie und phänomenologischen Philosophie* (1913; 3 Vols., Vols. III, IV, and V of *Husserliana* published 1950 sqq. at The Hague) and *Cartesianische Meditationen und Pariser Vorträge* (*Husserliana,* Vol. I, The Hague, 1950).

16. Cf. Husserl's retrospective characterization of this approach as embodied already in his *Philosophie der Arithmetik,* Vol. I (Halle, 1891).

17. Cf. Husserl, *Die Krisis der Europäischen Wissenschaften und die transzendentale Phänomenologie* (*Husserliana,* Vol. VI, The Hague, 1962).

18. For a detailed discussion cf. Franz Josef Brecht, *Bewusstsein und Existenz* (Bremen, 1948).—Martin Buber, *Das Problem des Menschen* (Heidelberg, 1948).—Max Scheler, *Metaphysik und Kunst. Schriften aus dem Nachlass,* I (1933); *Die Wissensformen und die Gesellschaft* (Leipzig, 1926); and *Gesammelte Werke,* II (Bern, 1954 sqq.), p. 46.

19. Max Scheler, *Gesammelte Werke,* II (Bern, 1954 sqq), p. 46.

20. Max Scheler, *loc. cit.,* p. 385.

21. Max Scheler, *loc. cit.,* p. 391.

22. This is the main theme of Husserl's lectures on "the consciousness of temporality."

23. Cf. *Husserliana,* II, p. 262.

24. Cf. *loc. cit.,* p. 259.

25. Max Scheler, *Die Stellung des Menschen im Kosmos* (Darmstadt, 1928), p. 48.

26. Scheler, *loc. cit.,* p. 106.

27. Scheler, *loc. cit.,* p. 66.

27a. Scheler, *loc. cit.,* p. 83.

28. Scheler, *loc. cit.,* p. 96.

29. Scheler, *Metaphysik und Kunst. Schriften aus dem Nachlass* I (1933). Cf. also *Die Wissensformen und die Gesellschaft* (Leipzig, 1926).— H. Lützeler, *Der Philosoph Max Scheler* (Bonn, 1947).—It cannot be our task here to investigate whether and to what extent Scheler's opposition of "spirit" and "drive" was due to the influence of Schelling's speculation.

30. Cf. Erich Rothacker, *Max Schelers Durchbruch zur Wirklichkeit. Akademische Vorträge und Abhandlungen* (Bonn, 1949).

31. Cf. Scheler, *Die Stellung des Menschen im Kosmos* (Darmstadt, 1928), p. 11.

32. Scheler, *loc. cit.*, p. 110.

33. Cf. Franz Josef Brecht, *Bewusstsein und Existenz* (Bremen, 1948), p. 96.

34. Cf. Scheler's essay "Der Mensch im Weltalter des Ausgleichs" in his *Philosophische Weltanschauung* (Bonn, 1929).

35. Cf. Scheler, *loc. cit.*, p. 12.

36. Cf. Landgrebe, *Phänomenologie und Metaphysik* (Hamburg, 1949), p. 164 sqq.

37. Cf. Martin Heidegger, *Sein und Zeit* (first published in *Jahrbuch fur Philosophie und phänomenologische Forschung*, VIII. Halle, 1927; 9th ed., Halle, 1961). See bibliography for English translation.

38. Cf. Heidegger, *loc. cit.*, p. 46.

39. For a more detailed discussion of *Dasein* cf. Chap. II of this volume.

40. Cf. Heidegger, *Sein und Zeit*, p. 42 and *passim*.

41. Cf. E. Mounier, *Introduction aux existentialismes* (Paris, 1947). See bibliography for English translation. Also Max Müller, *Existenzphilosophie im geistigen Leben der Gegenwart* (Heidelberg, 1949).

42. Cf. Jean-Paul Sartre, *L'Etre et le Néant* (Paris, 1943). See bibliography for English translation.

43. Cf. Sartre's play *Les Mouches* (Paris, 1943) and his essay on "Descartes und die Freiheit" (Mainz, 1948). See bibliography for translation of *Les Mouches.*

44. Cf. Heidegger, *Kant und das Problem der Metaphysik* (1929; 2nd ed., Frankfurt, 1951); *Was ist Metaphysik?* (1929; 5th ed., Frankfurt, 1949); *Hölderlin und das Wesen der Dichtung* (1936; published in translation in *Existence and Being,* ed. Werner Brock; see bibliography); *Einführung in die Metaphysik* (Tübingen, 1953); *Vom Wesen des Grundes* (1929; 4th ed., Frankfurt, 1949); *Platos Lehre von der Wahrheit* (1942; Bern, 1947); *Über den "Humanismus"* (Frankfurt, 1949); *Holzwege* (Frankfurt, 1950); *Vorträge und Aufsätze* (Pfullingen, 1954); *Was heisst Denken?* (Tübingen, 1954); *Was ist das—die Philosophie?* (Pfullingen, 1956); *Der Satz vom Grund* (Pfullingen, 1958); *Erläuterungen zu Hölderlins Dichtung* (2nd ed., Frankfurt, 1951). See bibliography for English translations.

45. The continuity in the development of Heidegger's thinking is shown by A. Diemer, *Grundzüge Heideggerschen Philosophierens. Zeitschrift für philosophische Forschung,* V, 4 (1951).

46. Of special significance in this connection are the works of Louis Lavelle and Gabriel Marcel (see bibliography).

47. Cf. Hans Lipps, *Untersuchungen zur Phänomenologie der Erkenntnis* (Bonn, 1927).

48. Cf. Lipps, *loc. cit.,* p. 78 sqq.

49. Cf. Lipps, *loc. cit.,* p. 91.

50. Cf. Lipps, *loc. cit.,* p. 49. Cf. also Lipps's interpretation of the meaning of Goethe's exploration of nature in *Die Wirklichkeit des Menschen* (Frankfurt, 1954).

51. Cf. Lipps, *Untersuchungen zu einer hermeneutischen Logik* (Frankfurt, 1938).

52. Cf. Landgrebe, *Phänomenologie und Metaphysik* (Hamburg, 1949), p. 56 sqq.

53. Cf. M. Brelage, *Fundamentalanalyse und Regionalanalyse* (Dissertation, Köln, 1956).

54. Nicolai Hartmann, *Der Aufbau der realen Welt* (Berlin, 1940).

55. Hartmann, *Zur Grundlegung der Ontologie* (Berlin, 1935), p. 128 sqq.

56. Hartmann, *loc. cit.*

57. Hartmann, *Der Aufbau der realen Welt,* p. 373.

58. Hartmann, *loc. cit.,* p. 374.

59. Hartmann, *Neue Wege der Ontologie* (2nd ed., Stuttgart, 1947), p. 232. See bibliography for English translation.

60. Hartmann, *Der Aufbau der realen Welt,* p. 215.

61. Hartmann, *loc. cit.*

62. Cf. Landgrebe, *Seinsregionen und regionale Ontologien in Husserls Phänomenologie. Studium Generale,* IX, 6 (1956), p. 314 sqq.

63. Cf. the more detailed discussion in Landgrebe, *Phänomenologie und Metaphysik,* p. 10 sqq.

64. Cf. *infra,* p. 71 sq.

65. Cf. *Husserliana,* Vol. III, p. 57 sq.

66. Cf. *Husserliana,* Vol. VI, p. 105 sqq.

67. Cf. Hartmann, *Der Aufbau der realen Welt,* p. 214.

68. Cf. *infra,* p. 97.

69. Cf. *infra,* p. 114 sqq.

70. Cf. Maurice Merleau-Ponty, *Phénoménologie de la Perception* (Paris, 1945). (See bibliography for English translation.) This meaning of the "bracketing" of the general thesis of the "world" is clearly articulated in the phenomenological analyses of Merleau-Ponty which are based on the results of *Gestalt*-psychology.

71. Cf. especially the pertinent investigations in several volumes of the *Husserliana.*

72. Cf. *supra,* p. 31 sq.

73. Cf. *supra,* p. 44 sq.

74. Cf. Heidegger, *Sein und Zeit,* p. 65.

75. Cf. Heidegger, *Vom Wesen des Grundes,* p. 19.

76. Cf. Heidegger, *loc. cit.*, p. 39 sq. and N. Hartmann, *Teleologisches Denken* (Berlin, 1951), p. 83 sqq.

77. Cf. Heidegger, *Sein und Zeit,* p. 135.

78. Cf. Heidegger, *loc. cit.*

79. Cf. Erwin Straus, *Vom Sinn der Sinne* (Berlin, 1935). The interrelation of sensation and movement has been explored by von Weizsäcker. Cf. Victor von Weizsäcker, *Der Gestaltkreis* (2nd ed., Leipzig, 1943) and Lipps, *Untersuchungen zur Phänomenologie der Erkenntnis* (Bonn, 1927), p. 74 sq.

80. Cf. M. Wundt, *Kant als Metaphysiker* (Stuttgart, 1924). J. Ebbinghaus, *Kantinterpretation und Kantkritik.* In *Deutsche Vierteljahrsschrift für Literaturwissenschaft und Geistesgeschichte,* I, 1924. Heidegger, *Kant und das Problem der Metaphysik.*

81. Cf. Chap. IV of this volume.

82. Cf. Carl Friedrich von Weizsäcker, *Zum Weltbild der Physik* (Leipzig, 1944), p. 84 and 96 sqq. See bibliography for English translation.

83. Cf. *Husserliana, passim.*

84. Cf. Hans Driesch in *Handbuch der Philosophie,* edited by Baeumler und Schröter (4 Vols., 1927-1935, Abteilung II); and Hans Spemann, *Experimentelle Beiträge zu einer Theorie der Entwicklung* (Berlin, 1936).

85. Cf. Riesser, *Merkmale des Zellebens, Universitas,* III, 9.

86. Cf. Richard Woltereck, *Philosophie der legendigen Wirklichkeit* (Vol. I: *Grundzüge einer allgemeinen Biologie;* Vol. II: *Ontologie des Lebendigen* (2nd ed., Stuttgart, 1940).

87. Cf. Ludwig von Bertalanffy, *Die organismische Auffassung und ihre Auswirkungen. Der Biologe,* 10 (1941); and Hermann Dotterweich, *Das biologische Gleichgewicht und seine Bedeutung für die Hauptprobleme der Biologie* (Jena, 1940).

88. Cf. Theodor Ballauf, *Das Problem des Lebendigen* (Bonn, 1949). Has a comprehensive bibliography.

89. Helmut Plessner, *Die Stufen des Organischen und der Mensch* (Bonn, 1928); and *Mensch und Tier* (Hamburg, 1946).

90. Cf. Ballauf, *loc. cit.;* and Jacob von Uexküll, *Bedeutungslehre* (Leipzig, 1940); *Die Lebenslehre: Das Weltbild,* Vol. 13 (Zürich, 1926-27); *Der Sinn des Lebens* (Godesberg, 1947). Also Gehlen, *Der Mensch,* p. 64 sqq.

91. Cf. Konrad Lorenz, *Die angeborenen Formen möglicher Erfahrung. Zeitschrift für Tierpsychologie,* V, 1 (1942), p. 274 sqq.; and *Über tanzähnliche Bewegungsweisen bei Tieren. Studium Generale,* V, 1 (1952), p. 1 sqq.

92. Cf. *supra,* p. 69 sq.

93. Cf. Hedwig Conrad-Martius, *Der Selbstaufbau der Natur* (Hamburg, 1944). The author questions and criticizes this presupposition of Driesch.

94. Aloys Wenzel, *Wissenschaft und Weltanschauung* (Leipzig, 1936), p. 123.

95. Carl Friedrich von Weizsäcker, *loc. cit.,* p. 86 sq.

96. C. F. v. Weizsäcker, *loc. cit.,* p. 90.

97. C. F. v. Weizsäcker, *loc. cit.,* p. 91.

98. C. F. v. Weizsäcker, *Beziehungen der theoretischen Physik zum Denken Heideggers* (in Carlos Astrada, Kurt Bauch, Ludwig Binswanger, and others, *Martin Heideggers Einfluss auf die Wissenschaften,* Bern, 1949).

99. Erwin Schrödinger, *Was ist Leben?* (Sammlung Dalp, 2nd ed., 1951). See bibliography for English translation.

100. Cf. Wilhelm Hoffmann, *Physik und Metaphysik. Symposion,* II (Freiburg, 1949), p. 353 sqq.

101. C. F. v. Weizsäcker, *Die Geschichte der Natur* (Göttingen, 1948), p. 90 sqq. See bibliography for English translation.

102. C. F. v. Weizsäcker, *loc. cit.;* also Schrödinger, *loc cit.,* p. 96 and 114 sqq.

103. Cf. *supra,* p. 79 sqq.

104. Cf. *supra,* p. 82.

105. This is the title of an unpublished manuscript.

106. Cf. *Das Wesen des Kunstwerks* in Heidegger's *Holzwege.*

107. Heidegger, *Über den Humanismus,* p. 23 sqq.

108. Cf. *supra,* pp. 46 sqq. and 77 sqq. of this volume.

109. Cf. Karl Löwith, *Weltgeschichte und Heilsgeschehen.* (Stuttgart, 1953). The fact that the Christian idea of a teleology in history has its roots in the Old Testament, can be disregarded in this context, for it was only owing to the influence of Christianity that this idea became a formative force in the West.

110. Cf. Wilhelm Dilthey, *Gesammelte Schriften,* Vols. 1-9, 11, 12 (Leipzig, 1923-1936), esp. Vol. 2.

111. Among those following Dilthey's lead, cf. especially Georg Misch, *Lebensphilosophie und Phänomenologie* (Bern, 1930) and *Geschichte der Autobiographie* (Bern, 3rd ed., 1949-50).—Bernhard Groethuysen, *Anthropologie* (in *Handbuch der Philosophie,* ed. Baeumler and Schröter, Vol. III).—Erich Rothacker, *Einleitung in die Geisteswissenschaften* (Tübingen, 1930); *Logik und Systematik der Geisteswissenschaften* (in *Handbuch,* II, 1927); *Geschichtsphilosophie* (in *Handbuch,* IV, 1930); *Probleme der Kulturanthropologie* (Bonn, 1948); *Mensch und Geschichte* (Bonn, 1950.—Joachim Wach, *Das Verstehen. Grundzüge einer Geschichte der hermeneutischen Theorien im 19. Jahrhundert,* 3 Vols. (Tübingen, 1926-1929).

112. For a more detailed discussion of the significance of the "*Südwestdeutsche Schule*" cf. Wilhelm Windelband's *Rektoratsrede* of 1894, titled *Geschichte und Naturwissenschaft* in Windelband's *Präludien* (9th ed., Tübingen, 1924), p. 136 sqq.; also Heinrich Rickert's summary discussion in his *Kulturwissenschaft und Naturwissenschaft* (5th ed., Tübingen, 1921).

113. Cf. Dilthey, *Gesammelte Schriften,* 12 vols. (new ed. Stuttgart and Göttingen, 1913-1958), *passim.*

114. Cf. Dilthey's address on the occasion of his 70th birthday in *Gesammelte Schriften,* VIII, p. 218 sqq.

115. Dilthey, *loc. cit.,* VII, p. 101.

116. Dilthey, *loc. cit.,* VIII.

117. Cf. *Handbuch der Philosophie,* IV.

118. Cf. Gehlen, *Urmensch and Spätkultur* (Bonn, 1956).

119. Cf. *supra,* p. 21 sqq. of this volume.

120. Arnold Toynbee, *A Study of History,* 12 vols. (London, New York: Oxford University Press, 1948-61).

121. Although Toynbee uses the term "civilization" in a manner that differs from our own terminology, he associates with it the identical meaning. What he has in mind is what Rothacker calls *Hochkultur* (cf. *Probleme der Kulturanthropologie* (Bonn, 1948).

122. Cf. *supra,* p. 44 sqq. and p. 77 sqq. of this volume.

123. Cf. the more explicit discussion of this concept in Chapt. VII of this volume, p. 171 sqq.

124. Hans Greyer, *Weltgeschichte Europas* (Wiesbaden, 1948).

125. Cf. Chapt. VI of this volume.

126. Wilhelm Dilthey, *Gesammelte Schriften,* VI, p. 104.

127. Immanuel Kant, *Kritik der Urteilskraft,* ¶ 46.

128. Cf. Charles Lalo *L'art et la vie,* 3 Vols. (Vrin, 1942-1947). In this work the author examines the interrelation of art and life in different historical epochs, with respect to the underlying conditioning sociological forces. He also distinguishes between different "types" of artists. As far as speculation on the philosophy of art is concerned, a number of articles in the *Journal of Aesthetics and Art Criticism* (ed. by Thomas Munro, 1941 sqq., Baltimore, American Society for Aesthetics) follow the same traditional and conventional trend of thought. They examine the creative artistic process with special emphasis on its relation to psychological and sociological conditioning forces and make an attempt at a "typological" description of the artistic creation, which is seen as a purely "natural" phenomenon, analogous to the processes of nature, with total disregard of any metaphysical horizon and without any reference to the problem of "truth."

129. An attempt to apply these basic principles to the philosophy of art was made by Hans-Hermann Groothoff in his *Untersuchungen über die philosophische Wesensbestimmung der Kunst bei Plato und Aristoteles und ihre Bedeutung für die neuzeitliche Poetik und Philosophie der Kunst* (Dissertation, Kiel, 1951). Following some suggestions of Heidegger, Beda Allemann (cf. *Über das Dichterische,* Zürich, 1956) has demanded that the tasks and problems of *Literaturwissenschaft* be understood as an inquiry into the "inner historicity" of this discipline; in addition, Allemann has attempted to arrive at a historical concept of "poetic rhythm."

130. Cf. Dilthey, *loc. cit.,* VI, p. 185.

131. Cf. *supra,* p. 108 sq.

132. Cf. Dilthey, *loc. cit.,* p. 185.

133. Cf. Dilthey, *loc. cit.,* p. 230.

134. Cf. Dilthey, *loc. cit.,* p. 237.

135. Cf. Dilthey, *loc. cit.,* p. 230.

136. Cf. *supra,* p. 111.

137. Cf. especially R. Unger and his school (see Bibliography). Significant problems of methodology in their relation to the problem of "form" are discussed in the Introduction to P. Böckmann's *Formgeschichte der deutschen Dichtung,* I (see Bibliography).

138. See Bibliography.

139. See Bibliography.

140. Cf. Max Scheler, *Metaphysik und Kunst. Schriften aus dem Nachlass,* I, 1933; also Scheler's *Die Wissensformen und die Gesellschaft* (Leipzig, 1926); and *supra,* p. 37 sqq.

141. Cf. Moritz Geiger, *Beiträge zur Phänomenologie des ästhetischen Genusses. Jahrbuch für Philosophie und phänomenologische Forschung,* I, 2 (1914).

142. Cf. Geiger, *Zugänge zur Asthetik* (Leipzig, 1928), p. 114.

143. Cf. Geiger, *loc. cit.,* p. 134.

144. Cf. Chap. VI.

145. Cf. Fritz Kaufmann, *Die Bedeutung der künstlerischen Stimmung,* in *Husserl-Festschrift* (Halle, 1929).

146. Cf. *supra,* p. 79 sqq.

147. See Bibliography.

148. Cf. *supra,* p. 53 sq.

149. Cf. Emil Staiger, *Die Zeit als Einbildungskraft des Dichters* (Zürich, 1946).

150. Cf. Staiger, *Poetik* (Zürich, 1948). See Bibliography.

151. See Bibliography.

152. Cf. *supra,* p. 77 sqq.

153. Cf. Kurt Riezler, *Traktat vom Schönen* (Frankfurt, 1935).

154. Cf. Riezler, *loc cit.,* p. 71.

155. Cf. Riezler, *loc. cit.,* p. 202.

156. Cf. Heidegger, *Was ist Metaphysik?*

157. Cf. Heidegger, *Holzwege,* p. 35.

158. Cf. Heidegger, *loc. cit.,* pp. 44, 49, 50.

159. The problem of "humanism" is further discussed *infra,* p. 156 sqq. and p. 172 sq.

160. Cf. Max Weber's celebrated essay, *Wissenschaft als Beruf* in *Gesammelte Aufsätze zur Wissenschaftslehre* (Tübingen, 1922).

161. Cf. Windelband-Heimsoeth, *Lehrbuch der Geschichte der Philosophie* (15th ed., Tübingen, 1957), especially the last chapter, entitled *Die Philosophie im 20. Jahrhundert* (with a comprehensive bibliographical survey to 1955), p. 569.

162. Cf. for example E. Jordan, *The Role of Philosophy in Social Crisis* in the journal *Ethics* (University of Chicago Press), July, 1941, p. 390 sqq.

163. Cf. R. Le Senne, *Traité de morale générale* (Paris, 1947).

164. Cf. Raymond Polin, *La création des valeurs* (Paris, 1944).

165. Cf. Theodor Steinbüchel, *Religion und Moral im Lichte personaler christlicher Existenz* (Frankfurt a.M., 1951).

166. Cf. Gabriel Marcel, *Etre et avoir* (Paris, 1935), especially the section entitled *Remarques sur l'irreligion contemporaine,* which discusses the interrelation of technology and epistemology. (See bibliography for English translation.) Cf. also E. Mounier (See bibliography).

167. Cf. G. Bastide, *De la condition humaine* (Paris, 1939).

168. Cf. W. Stace, *The Destiny of Western Man* (New York: Reynal and Hitchcock, 1942).

169. Cf. R. Flewelling, *Thè Survival of Western Culture* (New York: Harper and Bros., 1943).

170. Cf. Eugène Dupréel, *Esquisse d'une philosophie des valeurs* (Paris, 1939).

171. Cf. the references to Ortega Y. Gasset *infra,* p. 162 sq.

172. Cf. the discussion of the philosophic and historical significance of these developments by the following authors: Karl Löwith, *Von Hegel zu Nietzsche* (see Bibliography); Maurice Merleau-Ponty, *Humanisme et terreur* (Paris, 1947); Ludwig Landgrebe, *Hegel und Marx. Marxismus-Studien,* I; and R. Heiss, *Hegel und Marx. Symposion,* I (1949).

173. Cf. especially Max Scheler, *Die Wissensformen und die Gesellschaft* (Leipzig, 1926).

174. Cf. *supra,* p. 111.

175. Cf. Ernst Troeltsch, *Die Sozialphilosophie des Christentums* (3rd ed., Tübingen, 1923) and Max Weber, *Die protestantische Ethik und der Geist des Kapitalismus* in Weber's *Gesammelte Aufsätze zur Religionssoziologie* I (Tübingen, 1921 sqq). (See bibliography for English translations.)

176. Cf. *supra,* p. 40.

177. Cf. Scheler, *Die Wissensformen und die Gesellschaft* (Leipzig, 1926), p. 79. The interconnections between the concept of the Deity in the later Middle Ages and the rise of natural science are discussed by H. Blumenberg in two essays, entitled *Der Kopernikanische Umsturz und die*

Weltstellung des Menschen: Eine Studie zum Zusammenhang von Naturwissenschaft und Geistesgeschichte (in *Studium Generale*, VIII, 10 (1955), pp. 637 sqq.; and *Kosmos und System: Aus der Genesis der Kopernikanischen Welt* (*loc. cit.*, X, 2 (1957), p. 67 sqq.

178. Cf. Franz Brentano, *Vom Ursprung sittlicher Erkenntnis. Philosophische Bibliothek* (3rd ed., Leipzig, 1934).

179. Cf. Nicolai Hartmann, *Grundzüge einer Metaphysik der Erkenntnis* (4th ed., Berlin, 1949), p. 535.

180. Cf. Scheler, *loc. cit.*, p. 139.

181. Cf. Scheler, *loc. cit.*, p. 143.

182. Cf. Scheler, *loc. cit.*, p. 147.

183. Cf. Scheler, *loc. cit.*, p. 484.

184. Cf. Scheler, *loc. cit.*, p. 245.

185. Cf. Heidegger, *Platos Lehre von der Wahrheit* (Bern, 1947). The important question in our context does not ask whether Heidegger's interpretation is valid in every detail or whether certain tenets of Western "humanism" are perhaps erroneously attributed to Plato. What really matters is Heidegger's recognition that even in the earliest stages of Western metaphysics the total amplitude of its future historical evolution was already potentially contained.

186. Cf. the "Philological Postscript" in Karl Schlechta's new edition of Nietzsche's works in 3 Vols. (München: Carl Hanser, 1956), Vol. 3, pp. 1383-1432. Cf. also Heidegger's interpretation of Nietzsche in the essay entitled *Nietzsches Wort "Gott ist tot"* (in *Holzwege*, pp. 193-247); and especialy in Heidegger's probably definitive work, *Nietzsche*, 2 Vols. (Pfullingen: Neske, 1961).

187. Cf. Heidegger, *Holzwege*, p. 215.

188. Cf. Heidegger, *loc. cit.*, p. 221.

189. Cf. Heidegger, *Über den Humanismus*. See Bibliography.

190. Cf. *supra*, p. 47 sq. and p. 118 sq.

191. Cf. *infra*, p. 177 sqq.

192. Cf. especially Ortega Y Gasset's essays listed in the Bibliography.

193. Cf. Ortega's essays listed in the Bibliography; and Julián Marías, *José Ortega y Gasset and the Idea of Vital Reason* (1952).

194. Cf. Josef Pieper, *Muße und Kult* (München, 1955). See bibliography for English translation.

195. Cf. Pieper, *loc. cit.*, p. 67 sq.

196. Cf. also H. G. Gadamer, *Zur Vorgeschichte der Metaphysik* (in *Anteile. Martin Heidegger zum 60. Geburtstag.* Frankfurt, a.M., 1950), p. 51 sqq.

197. Cf. Etienne Gilson *L'Etre et l'essence* (Paris, 1948).

198. Cf. for example Josef Gredt, O.S.B., *Die aristotelisch-thomistiche Philosophie* (Freiburg i.B., 1935); or Caspar Ninck, S.J., *Philosophische Gotteslehre* (München, 1948).

199. Cf. Max Müller, *Existenzphilosophie im geistigen Leben der Gegenwart* (Heidelberg, 1949), p. 23.

200. Cf. also M. Wundt, *Die deutsche Schulmetaphysik im 17. Jahrhundert* (Tübingen, 1939); and *Die deutsche Schulphilosophie im Zeitalter der Aufklärung* (Tübingen, 1945).

201. Cf. Josef Pieper, *Wahrheit der Dinge* (München, 1947), p. 76 sqq.

202. Cf. Ninck, *loc. cit.*

203. Cf. *supra,* p. 118 sq.

204. Cf. Heidegger, *Holzwege,* p. 179.

205. Cf. Heidegger, *loc. cit.*, p. 187.

206. Cf. *supra,* p. 156 sqq.

207. Heidegger, *Was ist Metaphysik?* Cf. the Introduction to the 5th ed., p. 7.

208. Cf. Heidegger, *loc. cit.*, p. 8.

209. Cf. Heidegger, *loc. cit.*, p. 19.

210. Cf. Heidegger, *loc. cit.*, p. 19.

211. Cf. Heidegger, *Nietzsches Wort "Gott ist tot"* in *Holzwege,* pp. 193-247.

212. Cf. Heidegger, *Holzwege,* p. 309.

213. Cf. Max Müller, *loc. cit.,* p. 69 sqq.

214. Cf. especially the writings of Louis Lavelle (see Bibliography).

215. Cf. Karl Jaspers, *Der philosophische Glaube* (München-Zürich, 1948).

216. Cf. Jaspers, *Wahrheit und Unheil der Bultmannschen Entmythologisierung* (in *Kerygma und Mythos,* III, 1954). In this controversial polemic tract Jaspers denounces any positively determined and rationally definable theological position as "illiberal orthodoxy."

217. Cf. Jaspers, *Vom Ursprung und Ziel der Geschichte* (München, 1950). See bibliography for English translation.

218. Cf. Heidegger, *Über den Humanismus,* p. 36 sq.

219. Cf. the pertinent observations of Max Müller (*op. cit., passim*).

220. Cf. Heidegger, *Holzwege,* p. 247.

221. Cf. Heidegger, *loc. cit.,* p. 308.

222. Cf. Helmut Kuhn, *Begegnung mit dem Sein. Meditationen zur Metaphysik* (Tübingen, 1954).

223. Cf. Heidegger, *Was ist Metaphysik?* (5th ed.), p. 18.

A. *General Bibliographical Reference Works*

Bibliographie de la Philosophie. Edited by the *Institut International de Philosophie* (Paris). Contains semi-annual listings and analyses of works published since 1938, including articles published in periodicals and professional journals.

Bibliographische Einführungen in das Studium der Philosophie. Edited by İ. M. Bocheński (Bern: A Francke, 1948 sqq.).

De Brie, *Bibliographia Philosophica* (Utrecht-Brüssel: Editiones Spectrum, 1933-1945).

Handbuch der Philosophie. 4 Vols. Edited by A. Baeumler and M. Schröter (München: Oldenbourg, 1927-1935).

Philosophie: Chronique des années de guerre, 1939-1945 (Paris: Hermann et Cie., 1950).

Répertoire bibliographique de la Philosophie. (Louvain: Éditions de l'Institut Supérieur de Philosophie). Continuation of the *Répertoire bibliographique* which appeared quarterly since 1934 in supplement to the *Revue néoscolastique de philosophie,* which became the *Revue philosophique de Louvain* in 1946.

Sciacca, M. F. *Italienische Philosophie der Gegenwart* (Bern: A. Francke, 1948). Bibliographical introductions to the study of philosophy.

B. *Selected Bibliography of the Most Significant Works of Contemporary European Philosophy and Philosophers*

Adorno, Theodor W. *Zur Metakritik der Erkenntnistheorie* (Stuttgart; 1956).

Allemann, Beda. *Hölderlin und Heidegger* (Zürich, 1954).

———. *Über das Dichterische* (Zürich, 1954).

Anderle, Othmar. *Das universalhistorische System A. J. Toynbees.* In *Die Universität,* LIII (Frankfurt a.M.).

Baeumler, Alfred. *Asthetik.* In *Handbuch der Philosophie,* III (München, 1927-1935).

———. *Kants Kritik der Urteilskraft* (Halle, 1923).

Ballauf, Theodor. *Das Problem des Lebendigen. Eine Übersicht über den Stand der Forschung* (Bonn, 1949). Contains an extensive bibliography.

Barnes, Harry Elmer. *Soziologie der Geschichte.* In *Die Universität* (Wien-Stuttgart, 1951). Provides orientation on the research done on the Philosophy of History in the Anglo-Saxon countries.

Bastide, Georges. *De la condition humaine* (Paris, 1939).

Bavink, Bernhard. *Ergebnisse und Probleme der Naturwissenschaften* (7th ed., Leipzig, 1941). Translated from the 4th German edition as *The Natural Sciences* by H. Stafford Hatfield (New York: Century, 1932).

Becker, Oskar. *Die Hinfälligkeit des Schönen und die Abenteuerlichkeit des Künstlers. Husserl-Festschrift* (Halle, 1929).

Berger, Gaston. *The Different Trends of Contemporary French Philosophy. Philosophy and Phenomenological Research,* VII, 1 (1946), pp. 1-82.

Bertalanffy, Ludwig von. *Die organismische Auffassung und ihre Auswirkungen.* In *Der Biologe,* X (1941).

Bocheński, I. M. *Europäische Philosophie der Gegenwart* (Bern, 1947). Translated from the 2nd revised German edition as *Contemporary European Philosophy* by Donald Nicholl and Karl Aschenbrenner (Berkeley and Los Angeles: University of California Press, 1956).

———. *Der sowjetrussische dialektische Materialismus* (3rd ed., Bern, 1960).

Böckmann, Paul. *Formgeschichte der deutschen Dichtung,* I (Hamburg, 1949).

Bollnow, O. F. *Dilthey. Einführung in seine Philosophie* (2nd ed., revised, Stuttgart, 1955).

———. *Einfache Sittlichkeit* (Göttingen, 1947).

Brand, Gerd. *Ich, Welt und Zeit. Nach unveröffentlichten Manuskripten Edmund Husserls* (The Hague, 1955).

Brecht, Franz Josef. *Bewusstsein und Existenz* (Bremen, 1948).

Brentano, Franz. *Vom Ursprung sittlicher Erkenntnis.* (3rd ed., Leipzig, 1934).

Breysig, Kurt. *Der Stufenbau und die Gesetze der Weltgeschichte* (Stuttgart, 1927).

Broglie, Louis de. *Licht und Materie* (Hamburg, 1944). Translated as *Matter and Light* by W. H. Johnston (New York: Dover Publications, 1946).

———. *Physik und Mikrophysik* (Hamburg, 1950). Translated as *Physics and Microphysics* by Martin Davidson. With a foreword by A. Einstein. (New York: Pantheon Books, 1955).

Buber, Martin. *Das Problem des Menschen* (Heidelberg, 1948).

Camus, Albert. *Le Mythe de Sisyphe.* (Paris, 1942). Translated as *The Myth of Sisyphus* by Justin O'Brien (New York: Alfred A. Knopf, 1955).

———. *L'Homme révolté* (Paris, 1951). Translated as *The Rebel* by Anthony Bower. With a preface by Sir Herbert Read. (New York: Alfred A. Knopf, 1954; Vintage, 1956).

Collingwood, R. G. *The Idea of History* (Oxford: Clarendon Press, 1946; New York: Oxford University Press, 1956).

Conrad-Martius, Hedwig. *Der Selbstaufbau der Natur* (Hamburg, 1944).

Daniélou, Jean. *Essai sur le Mystère de l'Histoire* (Paris, 1953).

Diemer, Alwin. *Grundzüge Heideggerschen Philosophierens.* In *Zeitschrift für philosophische Forschung,* V, 4 (1951).

———. *Edmund Husserl. Versuch einer systematischen Darstellung seiner Philosophie* (Meisenheim, 1956).

Dilthey, Wilhelm. *Das Erlebnis und die Dichtung* (first published in 1905; 13th ed., Stuttgart, 1957).

———. *Gesammelte Schriften,* 12 Vols. (Stuttgart-Göttingen, 1913-1958).

Dotterweich, Hermann. *Das biologische Gleichgewicht und seine Bedeutung für die Hauptprobleme der Biologie* (Jena, 1940).

Driesch, Hans. *Metaphysik der Natur.* In *Handbuch der Philosophie,* II (ed. Baeumler und Schröter, 4 Vols., München, 1927-1935).

———. *The Science and Philosophy of the Organism* (Gifford Lectures, 1907-08; first published in English, London, A & C Black, 1908. German edition: *Philosophie des Organischen,* Leipzig, 1921).

Dufrenne, Mikel. *Phénoménologie de l'Expérience Esthétique* (Paris, 1953).

——— and Ricoeur, Paul. *Karl Jaspers et la philosophie de l'existence.* Préface de Karl Jaspers. (Paris, 1947).

Dupréel, Eugène. *Esquisse d'une philosophie des valeurs* (Paris, 1939).

Ebbinghaus, J. *Kantinterpretation und Kantkritik.* In *Deutsche Vierteljahrsschrift für Literaturwissenschaft und Geistesgeschichte* I, 1924.

Fiedler, Konrad. *Der Ursprung der künstlerischen Tätigkeit* (München, 1887).
Flewelling, Ralph Tyler. *The Survival of Western Culture* (New York: Harper and Bros., 1943).
Freyer, Hans. *Weltgeschichte Europas* (Wiesbaden, 1948).
Gadamer, Hans-Georg. *Plato und die Dichter* (Frankfurt, 1934).
Gehlen, Arnold. *Der Mensch* (4th ed., Bonn, 1950).
———. *Urmensch und Spätkultur* (Bonn, 1956).
Geiger, Moritz. *Beiträge zür Phänomenologie des ästhetischen Genusses. Jahrbuch für Philosophie und phänomenologische Forschung,* I, 2 (1914).
———. *Zugänge zur Asthetik* (Leipzig, 1928).
Gentile, Giovanni. *Philosophie der Kunst* (Berlin, 1934). Translated from the Italian by Heinrich Langen.
Gilson, Etienne. *L'Etre et l'Essence* (Paris, 1948).
———. *Being and Some Philosophers* (2nd ed. corrected and enlarged, Toronto: Pontifical Institute of Mediaeval Studies, 1952).
Grassi Ernesto and Uexküll, Thure V., eds. *Die Einheit unseres Wirklichkeitsbildes und die Grenzen der Einzelwissenschaften. Mit Beiträgen von Gerlach, Grassi, Portmann, Bally und Szilasi* (Hamburg, 1955).
Gredt, Josef. *Die Aristotelisch-thomistische Philosophie* (Freiburg, i.B., 1935).
Groethuysen, Bernhard. *Anthropologie.* In *Handbuch der Philosophie,* III (ed. Baeumler und Schröter, 4 Vols., München, 1927-1935).
Groothoff, Hans-Hermann. *Untersuchungen über die philosophische Wesensbestimmung der Kunst bei Plato und Aristoteles und ihre Bedeutung für die neuzeitliche Poetik und Philosophie der Kunst* (Dissertation, Kiel, 1951).
Guardini, Romano. *Welt und Person* (Würzburg, 1940).
———. *Freiheit, Gnade, Schicksal* (München, 1949).
Gurwitsch, Aron. *Théorie du champ de la Conscience* (Paris, 1957).
Häberlin, Paul. *Der Mensch* (Zürich, 1941).
Hartmann, Max. *Atomphysik, Biologie und Religion* (Stuttgart, 1947).
Hartmann, Nicolai. *Grundzüge einer Metaphysik der Erkenntnis* (Berlin, 1921; 4th ed., 1949).
———. *Ethik* (Berlin, 1926; 3rd ed., 1949). Translated from the German as *Ethics* by Stanton Coit (authorized version). (London: Allen & Unwin; New York: Macmillan, 1932).

———. *Das Problem des geistigen Seins* (Berlin, 1933; 2nd ed., 1949).

———. *Zur Grundlegung der Ontologie* (Berlin, 1935).

———. *Möglichkeit und Wirklichkeit* (Berlin, 1938).

———. *Der Aufbau der realen Welt* (Berlin, 1940).

———. *Neue Wege der Ontologie* (2nd ed., Stuttgart, 1947). Translated as *New Ways of Ontology* by Reinhard C. Kuhn (Chicago: H. Regnery Co., 1953).

———. *Philosophie der Natur* (Berlin, 1950).

———. *Teleologisches Denken* (Berlin, 1951).

———. *Ästhetik* (Berlin, 1953).

Hegel, G. W. F. *Phänomenologie des Geistes* (2nd ed., Berlin, 1841). Translated as *The Phenomenology of Mind,* with an introduction and notes by J. B. Baillie (2nd ed., rev., New York: Macmillan, 1931).

Heidegger, Martin. *Sein und Zeit.* First published in *Jahrbuch für Philosophie und phänomenologische Forschung,* VIII (Halle, 1927). Translated as *Being and Time* by John Macquarrie and Edward Robinson (London: SCM Press, 1962).

———. *Vom Wesen des Grundes* (1929; 4th ed., Frankfurt, 1949).

———. *Kant und das Problem der Metaphysik* (1929; 2nd ed., Frankfurt, 1951). Translated as *Kant and the Problem of Metaphysics* by James Churchill (Bloomington: Indiana University Press, 1962).

———. *Was ist Metaphysik?* (1929; mit einem Nachwort, 1943; citations in this volume relate to the 4th edition (Frankfurt, 1949). Translated as *What is Metaphysics?* by R. F. C. Hull and Alan Crick, in *Existence and Being.* Edited by Werner Brock (Chicago: Regnery, 1949), pp. 353-392.

———. *Hölderlin und das Wesen der Dichtung* (München, 1937). Translated as *Hölderlin and the Essence of Poetry* by Douglas Scott, in *Existence and Being.* Edited by Werner Brock (Chicago: Regnery, 1949), pp. 317-351.

———. *Platos Lehre von der Wahrheit* (1942; Bern, 1947).

———. *Vom Wesen der Wahrheit* (1943; 3rd ed., Frankfurt, 1954). Translated as *On the Essence of Truth* by R. F. C. Hull and Alan Crick in *Existence and Being.* Edited by Werner Brock (Chicago: Regnery, 1949), pp. 317-351).

———. *Über den Humanismus* (Frankfurt, 1949).

———. *Holzwege* (Frankfurt, 1950).

———. *Erläuterungen zu Hölderlings Dichtung* (2nd ed., Frankfurt, 1951).

———. *Einführung in die Metaphysik* (Tübingen, 1953). Translated as *Introduction to Metaphysics* by Ralph Manheim (New Haven: Yale University Press, 1958).

———. *Aus der Erfahrung des Denkens* (Pfullingen, 1954).

———. *Was heißt Denken* (Tübingen, 1954).

———. *Vorträge und Aufsätze* (Pfullingen, 1954).

———. *Was ist das—die Philosophie?* (Pfullingen, 1956). Translated as *What is Philosophy?* by W. Kluback and J. T. Wilde (New York: Twayne, 1948).

———. *Zur Seinsfrage* (Frankfurt, 1956). Translated as *The Question of Being* by W. Kluback and J. T. Wilde (New York: Twayne, 1959).

———. *Der Satz vom Grund* (Pfullingen, 1957).

———. *Nietzsche,* 2 Vols. (Pfullingen, 1961).

Heisenberg, Werner. *Wandlungen in den Grundlagen der Naturwissenschaft. Acht Vorträge* (Stuttgart, 1949).

Hoffmann, Wilhelm. *Physik und Metaphysik. Symposion,* II (Freiburg, 1949).

Hunger, Edgar. *Das naturwissenschaftliche Weltbild. Einführung und Quellensammlung,* I (Braunschweig, 1955).

Husserl, Edmund. *Husserliana. Gesammelte Werke* (The Hague: Martinus Nijhoff, 1950 sqq.). Contains most of the works published during Husserl's life time as well as those published posthumously. 9 Vols. have been published thus far.

———. *Philosophie der Arithmetik,* Vol. I (Halle, 1891).

———. *Logische Untersuchungen,* I and II (2nd ed., Halle, 1913, Bd. 1; 1921, Bd. 2).

———. *Philosophie als strenge Wissenschaft. Logos,* I, 1910.

———. *Die Idee der Phänomenologie. Fünf Vorlesungen.* Vol. II of *Husserliana* (2nd ed., The Hague, 1958). Translated as *The Idea of Phenomenology* by William P. Alston and George Nakhnikian (The Hague, 1964).

———. *Ideen zu einer reinen Phänomenologie und phänomenologischen Philosophie,* 3 Vols. Vols. III, IV, and V of *Husserliana* (The Hague, 1950 sqq.). Vol. I has been translated as *Ideas of a Pure Phenomenology,* by W. R. Boyce Gibson (New York: Macmillan, 1952).

———. *Cartesianische Meditationen und Pariser Vorträge.* Vol. I of *Husserliana* (2nd ed., The Hague, 1963). Translated as *Cartesian Meditations. An Introduction to Phenomenology,* by Dorion Cairns (The Hague, 1960).

———. *Vorlesungen zur Phänomenologie des inneren Zeitbewusstseins.* Edited by Martin Heidegger. *Jahrbuch für Philosophie und phänomenologische Forschung,* IX (Halle, 1928).

Translated as *The Phenomenology of Internal Time Consciousness* by James S. Churchill (Bloomington: Indiana University Press, 1964).

———. *Erfahrung und Urteil.* Edited by Ludwig Landgrebe (2nd ed., Hamburg, 1953).

Ingarden, Roman. *Das literarische Kunstwerk* (2nd ed., rev., Tübingen, 1960).

Jaspers, Karl. *Allgemeine Psychopathologie* (2nd ed., rev., Berlin, 1920). Translated as *General Psychopathology* by J. Hoenig and Marion W. Hamilton (Chicago: University of Chicago Press, 1963).

———. *Psychologie der Weltanschauungen* (Berlin, 1919).

———. *Die Idee der Universität* (Berlin, 1923). Translated as *The Idea of the University* by H. A. T. Reiche and H. F. Vanderschmidt. Edited by Karl W. Deutsch. Preface by Robert Ulich. (Boston: Beacon Press, 1959.

———. *Die geistige Situation der Zeit* (5th ed., Berlin, 1933). Translated as *Man in the Modern Age* by E. Paul (London: Routledge, 1959).

———. *Vernunft und Existenz* (Groningen, 1935). Translated as *Reason and Existence* by William Earle (New York: Noonday, 1955).

———. *Von der Wahrheit. Philosophische Logik,* I (München, 1947). The following translations are selections from *Von der Wahrheit: Tragedy is not enough,* translated by Harold Reiche, Harry Moore and Karl Deutsch (London: Gollancz, 1953); *Truth and Symbol,* translated with an introduction by Jean Wilde, William Kluback and William Kimmel (New York: Twayne, 1959).

———. *Philosophie,* 3 Vols. (Berlin, 1932; 2nd and sqq. ed., 1948 sqq.).

———. *Der philosophische Glaube* (München-Zürich, 1948). Translated as *The Perennial Scope of Philosophy* by Ralph Manheim (New York: Philosophical Library, 1949).

———. *Vom Ursprung und Ziel der Geschichte* (München, 1950). Translated as *The Origin and Goal of History* by Michael Bullock (New Haven: Yale University Press, 1953).

———. *Rechenschaft und Ausblicke. Reden und Aufsätze* (München, 1951).

———. *Einführung in die Philosophie* (Zürich, 1950). Translated as *Way to Wisdom* by Ralph Manheim (New Haven: Yale University Press, 1954).

———. *Wahrheit und Unheil der Bultmannschen Entmythologisierung.* In *Kerygma und Mythos,* III.

———. *Die grossen Philosophen,* Vol. I (München, 1957).

Translated as *The Great Philosophers* by Ralph Manheim. Edited by Hannah Arendt (New York: Harcourt, 1962).
Jeans, Sir James. *Physics and Philosophy* (Cambridge: University Press, 1942).
Jordan, Pascual. *Die Physik und das Geheimnis des Lebens* (6th ed., Braunschweig, 1948).
———. *Die Physik des 20. Jahrhunderts* (7th ed., Braunschweig, 1949).
Jünger, Ernst. *Der Arbeiter* (Hamburg, 1932).
Kaufmann, Fritz. *Die Bedeutung der künstlerischen Stimmung. Husserl-Festschrift* (Halle, 1929).
———. *Geschichtsphilosophie der Gegenwart. Philosophische Forschungsberichte,* X (1931).
Kayser, Wolfgang. *Das sprachliche Kunstwerk* (6th ed., Bern, 1960).
Kuhn, Helmut. *Begegnung mit dem Sein. Meditationen zur Metaphysik des Gewissens* (Tübingen, 1954).
Landgrebe, Ludwig. *Wilhelm Diltheys Theorie der Geisteswissenschaften* (Halle, 1928).
———. *Hegel und Marx. Marxismusstudien,* Vol. I (Tübingen, 1954).
———. *Phänomenologie und Metaphysik* (Hamburg, 1949).
———. *Das Problem der ursprünglichen Erfahrung im Werke von Hans Lipps.* In *Philosophische Rundschau,* IV, 3, 4 (1956).
———. *Seinsregionen und regionale Ontologien in Husserls Phänomenologie. Studium Generale* IX, 6 (1956).
Lange, Max G. *Marxismus, Leninismus, Stalinismus* (Stuttgart, 1955).
Lavelle, Louis. *La présence totale* (Paris, 1934).
———. *De l'acte* (Paris, 1937).
———. *La parole et l'écriture* (Paris, 1942).
———. *Du temps et de l'éternité* (Paris, 1945).
———. *Introduction à l'ontologie* (Paris, 1947).
———. *Traité des valeurs,* 2 Vols. (Paris, 1951, 1955).
Le Senne, René. *Traité de morale générale* (Paris, 1947).
Lipps, Hans. *Untersuchungen zur Phänomenologie der Erkenntnis* (Bonn, 1927).
———. *Untersuchungen zu einer hermeneutischen Logik* (Frankfurt, 1938).
———. *Die menschliche Natur* (Frankfurt, 1941).
———. *Die Verbindlichkeit der Sprache* (Frankfurt, 1944).
———. *Die Wirklichkeit des Menschen* (Frankfurt, 1954).
Litt, Theodor. *Wege und Irrwege geschichtlichen Denkens* (München, 1948).

Lorenz, Konrad. *Die angeborenen Formen möglicher Erfahrung. Zeitschrift für Tierpsychologie,* V (1962), p. 274 sqq.

———. *Über tanzähnliche Bewegungsweisen bei Tieren. Studium Generale,* V, 1 (1952).

Löwith, Karl. *Von Hegel zu Nietzsche* (Zürich, 1941). Translated as *From Hegel to Nietzsche* by David E. Green (New York: Holt, 1964).

———. *Weltgeschichte und Heilsgeschehen. Urban-Bücher* (Stuttgart, 1953).

Lützeler, H. *Der Philosoph Max Scheler* (Bonn, 1947).

Madinier, Gabriel. *La conscience morale* (Paris, 1958).

Marcel, Gabriel. *Etre et avoir* (Paris, 1935). Cf. especially the section titled *Remarques sur l'irreligion contemporaine* which deals with the interrelation of technology and epistemology. Translated as *Being and Having* by Katharine Farrer (Boston, 1951).

Marías-Aguilera, Julián. *Ortega y la idea de la razón vital* (Madrid, 1948).

———. *Ortega y tres antípodas; un ejemplo de intriga intelectual* (Buenos Aires, 1950).

Meinecke, Friedrich. *Die Entstehung des Historismus,* 2 Vols. (München, 1936).

Merleau-Ponty, Maurice. *Phénoménologie de la Perception* (Paris, 1945). Translated as *Phenomenology of Perception* by Colin Smith (New York: Humanities Press, 1962).

———. *Humanisme et terreur* (Paris, 1947).

———. *Sens et Non-sens* (Paris, 1948).

———. *Eloge de la Philosophie* (Paris, 1953).

———. *Les philosophes célèbres* (Paris, 1957).

Meyer, Rudolf W. *Merleau-Ponty un das Schicksal des französischen Existentialismus.* In *Philosophische Rundschau,* III, 3, 4 (1955, 1956).

Misch, Georg. *Lebensphilosophie und Phänomenologie* (Bonn, 1931).

———. *Geschichte der Autobiographie* (1st ed., 1907; 3rd ed., Bern, 1949, 1950). Translated as *A History of Autobiography in Antiquity* by Ernst Walter Dickes, in collaboration with the author. 2 Vols. (London: Routledge and Kegan Paul, 1950).

Möller, Joseph. *Existenzphilosophie und katholische Theologie* (Baden-Baden, 1952).

Mounier, Emanuel. *Introduction aux existentialismes* (Paris, 1947). Translated as *Existentialist Philosophies,* An Introduction, by Eric Blow (London: Rockliff, 1948).

Müller, Max. *Existenzphilosophie im geistigen Leben der Gegenwart* (2nd ed., rev., Heidelberg, 1958).
Müller-Vollmer, Kurt. *Towards a Phenomenological Theory of Literature. A Study of Wilhelm Dilthey's Poetik* (The Hague, 1963).
Ninck, Caspar. *Philosophische Gotteslehre* (München, 1948).
———. *Metaphysik des sittlich Guten* (Freiburg, 1955).
Nohl, Hermann. *Stil und Weltanschauung* (Jena, 1920).
———. *Die ästhetische Wirklichkeit* (Frankfurt, 1935).
———. *Die sittlichen Grunderfahrungen. Eine Einführung in die Ethik* (3rd ed., Frankfurt a.M., 1949).
Odebrecht, Rudolf. *Ästhetik der Gegenwart. Philosophische Forschungsberichte,* XV (1932).
Ortega y Gasset, José. *Obras completas,* 6 Vols. (Madrid, (1946-47).
———. *Die Krise der Vernunft* (in *Europäische Revue,* XVIII, 3). A translation of *Meditación de la técnica.*
———. *Man and Crisis.* Translated from *En torno a Galileo* by Mildred Adams (New York: Norton, 1958).
———. *Man and People.* Translated from *El hombre y la gente* by Willard R. Trask (New York: Norton, 1957).
Pfeiffer, Johannes. *Das lyrische Gedicht als äesthetisches Gebilde* (Halle, 1931).
———. *Existenzphilosophie. Eine Einführung in Heidegger und Jaspers* (Leipzig, 1933; 3rd ed., rev., Hamburg, 1952).
———. *Zwischen Dichtung und Philosophie* (Bremen, 1947).
———. *Sinn und Grenzen der Dichtung* (Bremen, 1947).
———. *Wege zur Dichtung* (Hamburg, 1952).
Pieper, Josef. *Wahrheit der Dinge* (München, 1951).
———. *Muße und Kult* (München, 1955). Translated as *Leisure: The Basis of Culture* by Alexander Dru. With an introduction by T. S. Eliot (New York: Pantheon Books, 1952).
Planck, Max. *Vorträge und Erinnerungen* (5th ed. of *Wege zur physikalischen Erkenntnis;* Stuttgart, 1949).
Plessner, Helmut. *Die Stufen des Organischen und der Mensch* Bonn, 1928).
———. *Mensch und Tier.* In *Gottfried Wilhelm Leibniz* (Hamburg, 1946).
Polin, Raymond. *La création des valeurs* (Paris, 1944).
Portmann, Adolf. *Das Problem des Lebens* (Basel, 1947).
Raeymaeker, Louis de. *Philosophie de l'Etre* (Louvain, 1947).
Renoirte, Fernand and Mercier, André. *Philosophie der exakten Wissenschaften* (Zürich-Köln, 1955).
Richardson, Wm. J., S.J. *Heidegger: Through Phenomenology to*

Thought. Preface by Martin Heidegger (The Hague: Martinus Nijhoff, 1963).

Rickert, Heinrich. *Kulturwissenschaft und Naturwissenschaft* (Lectures first published 1898; 5th and sqq. ed., Tübingen, 1921 sqq.).

———. *Die Grenzen der naturwissenschaftlichen Begriffsbildung* (Tübingen, 1902; 5th ed., 1929).

———. *Grundprobleme der philosophischen Methodologie, Ontologie, Anthropologie* (Tübingen, 1934).

———. *Science and History*. Translated by George Reisman. Edited by Arthur Goddard (Princeton: Van Nostrand, 1962).

Ricoeur. Paul. *Phénoménologie de la volonté* (Paris, 1949).

———. *Histoire et Verité* (Paris, 1955).

Riezler, Kurt. *Traktat vom Schönen* (Frankfurt, 1935).

Rothacker, Erich. *Einleitung in die Geisteswissenschaften* (2nd ed., Tübingen, 1930).

———. *Logik und Systematik der Geisteswissenschaften.* In *Handbuch der Philosophie,* II (München, 1927).

———. *Geschichtsphilosophie.* In *Handbuch der Philosophie,* IV (1930).

———. *Probleme der Kulturanthropologie* (Bonn, 1948).

———. *Mensch und Geschichte* (2nd ed., Bonn, 1950).

———. *Max Schelers Durchbruch zur Wirklichkeit. Akademische Vorträge und Abhandlungen* (Bonn, 1949).

Sartre, Jean-Paul. *L'Être et le néant: essai d'ontologie phénoménologique* (Paris, 1943). Translated as *Being and Nothingness* by Hazel E. Barnes (New York: Philosophical Library, 1956).

———. *L'Existentialisme est un humanisme* (Paris, 1945). Translated as *Existentialism* by Bernard Frechtman (New York: Philosophical Library, 1947).

———. *Qu'est-ce que la littérature?* (Paris, 1954). Translated as *What Is Literature?* by Bernard Frechtman (New York: Philosophical Library, 1949).

———. *Les Mouches* (Paris, 1943). Translated by Stuart Gilbert in: *No Exit,* a play in one act and *The Flies* (New York: Knopf, 1947).

———. *Morts sans sepulture* (Paris, 1947), translated as *The Victors; La putain respectueuse* (Paris, 1946), translated as *The Respectful Prostitute;* and *Les mains sales* (Paris, 1948), translated as *Dirty Hands* are collected in an edition of *Three Plays,* translated by Lionel Abel (New York: Knopf, 1949).

———. *"Descartes und die Freiheit"* (Mainz, 1948).

———. *Les chemins de la liberté.* (1) *L'Age de raison.* Trans. as *The Age of Reason* by Eric Sutton (New York: A. Knopf,

1952). (2) *Le Sursis.* Trans. as *The Reprieve* by Eric Sutton (London: Hamish Hamilton, 1947). (3) *La mort dans l'âme.* Trans. as *Troubled Sleep* by Gerard Hopkins (New York: A. Knopf, 1951).

Scheler, Max. *Wesen und Formen der Sympathie* (Enlarged and corrected ed., Bonn, 1923; original edition under the title: *Zur Phänomenologie und Theorie der Sympathiegefühle und von Liebe und Haß.* (Halle, 1914). Translated as *The Nature of Sympathy* by Peter Heath (London: Routledge and Kegan Paul, 1954).

———. *Vom Ewigen im Menschen* (Leipzig, 1921). Translated as *On the Eternal in Man* by Bernard Noble (New York: Harper, 1961).

———. *Die deutsche Philosophie der Gegenwart.* In *Deutsches Leben der Gegenwart,* ed. Ph. Witkop (Berlin, 1922).

———. *Die Wissensformen und die Gesellschaft* (Leipzig, 1926).

———. *Die Stellung des Menschen im Kosmos* (Darmstadt, 1928). Translated as *Man's Place in Nature* by Hans Meyerhoff, with an introduction. (Boston: Beacon Press, 1961).

———. *Philosophische Weltanschauung* (Bonn, 1929). Translated as *Philosophical Perspectives* by Oscar A. Haac (Boston: Beacon Press, 1958).

———. *Metaphysik und Kunst. Schriften aus dem Nachlass,* I (1933).

———. *Gesammelte Werke* (Bern, 1954 sqq.).

Schrödinger, Erwin. *Was ist Leben?* (2nd ed., Bern, 1951). Translated by L. Mazurczak from the original English, *What Is Life?* (New York: Macmillan, 1945).

Schulz, Walter. *Über den philosophiegeschichtlichen Ort Martin Heideggers.* In *Philosophische Rundschau,* I, 3, 4 (1953-1954).

———. *Der Gott der neuzeitlichen Metaphysik* (Pfullingen, 1957).

Spemann, Hans. *Experimentelle Beiträge zu einer Theorie der Entwicklung* (Berlin, 1936).

Spiegelberg, Herbert. *French existentialism: its social philosophies. Kenyon Review,* XVI (1954), 454-62.

———. *The Phenomenological Movement.* A Historical Introduction. 2 vols. (The Hague: Martinus Nijhoff, 1960).

Stace, W. T. *The Destiny of Western Man* (New York: Reynal and Hitchcock, 1942).

Staiger, Emil. *Die Zeit als Einbildungskraft des Dichters* (2nd ed., Zürich, 1953).

———. *Grundbegriffe der Poetik* (4th ed., Zürich, 1959).

———. *Die Kunst der Interpretation* (2nd ed., Zürich, 1957).
Stegmüller, Wolfgang. *Hauptströmungen der Gegenwartsphilosophie* (Wien-Stuttgart, 1952).
Steinbüchel, Theodor. *Religion und Moral im Lichte personaler christlicher Existenz* (Frankfurt, 1951).
Straus, Erwin. *Vom Sinn der Sinne* (Berlin, 1935).
Thienemann, August. *Leben und Umwelt. Bios,* XII (1941).
Toynbee, Arnold J. *A Study of History,* 12 Vols. (London-New York: Oxford University Press, 1948-61).
———. *Civilization on Trial* (New York: Oxford University Press, 1948).
Troeltsch, Ernst. *Der Historismus und seine Überwindung* (Berlin, 1924).
———. *Die Soziallehren der christlichen Kirchen und Gruppen* (3rd ed., Tübingen, 1923). Translated as *The Social Teachings of the Christian Churches* (New York: Macmillan, 1931).
Ueberweg, Friedrich. *Grundriss der Geschichte der Philosophie.* 4 Teil: *Die deutsche Philosophie des 19. Jahrhunderts und der Gegenwart* (13th ed., Tübingen, 1951).
Uexküll, Jacob von. *Bedeutungslehre* (Leipzig, 1940).
———. *Die Lebenslehre. Das Weltbild,* XIII (Zürich, 1926-27).
———. *Der Sinn des Lebens* (Godesberg, 1947).
Unger, Rudolf. *Literaturgeschichte als Problemgeschichte* (Berlin, 1924).
———. *Gesammelte Studien,* 2 Vols. (Berlin, 1929).
Utitz, Emil. *Geschichte der Ästhetik* (Berlin, 1932).
Varet, Gilbert. *L'Ontologie de Sartre* (Paris, 1948).
Wach, Joachim. *Das Verstehen. Grundzüge einer Geschichte der hermeneutischen Theorien im 19. Jahrhundert,* 3 Vols. (Tübingen, 1926-1929).
Waehlens, Alphonse de. *Une Philosophie de l'Ambiguité* (Louvain, 1951).
———. *Phénoménologie et Verité* (Paris, 1953).
Wagner, Hans. *Kritische Betrachtungen zu Husserls Nachlass.* In *Philosophische Rundschau,* I, 1 (1953, 1954).
Wahl, Jean. *Traité de Métaphysique* (Paris, 1933).
———. *Tableau de la philosophie française* (Paris, 1946).
Weber, Max. *Gesammelte Aufsätze zur Religionssoziologie* (Tübingen, 1921 sqq.).
———. *Die protestantische Ethik und der Geist des Kapitalismus.* In *Gesammelte Aufsätze zur Religionssoziologie.* Translated as *The Protestant Ethic and the Spirit of Capitalism* with a preface by R. H. Tawney (New York: Scribners, 1930).

———. *Gesammelte Aufsätze zur Wissenschaftslehre* (Tübingen, 1922).

Weil, Eric. *Philosophie politique* (Paris, 1956).

Weizsäcker, Carl Friedrich von. *Zum Weltbild der Physik* (Leipzig, 1944). Translated as *The World View of Physics* by Marjorie Grene (Chicago: University of Chicago Press, 1952).

———. *Die Geschichte der Natur* (Göttingen, 1948). Translated as *The History of Nature* by Fred D. Wieck (Chicago: University of Chicago Press, 1949).

———. *Beziehungen der theoretischen Physik zum Denken Heideggers.* In *Martin Heideggers Einfluß auf die Wissenschaften* by Carlos Astrada, Kurt Bauch, Ludw. Binswanger and others (Bern, 1949).

Weizsäcker, Victor von. *Der Gestaltkreis* (2nd ed., Leipzig, 1943).

Wenzl, Aloys. *Wissenschaft und Weltanschauung* (Leipzig, 1936).

———. *Metaphysik der Physik von heute.* In *Wissenschaft und Zeitgeist,* II (Leipzig, 1935).

———. *Metaphysik der Biologie von heute* (Leipzig, 1938).

———. *Materie und Leben* (Stuttgart, 1949).

Wetter, Gustav A. *Der dialektische Materialismus* (2nd ed., Freiburg, 1953).

Windelband, Wilhelm. *Präludien* (9th ed., Tübingen, 1924).

Windelband, Wilhelm and Heimsoeth, Heinz. *Lehrbuch der Geschichte der Philosophie* (15th ed., Tübingen, 1957). The last chapter discusses *Die Philosophie im 20. Jahrhundert* and traces the results of philosophico-historical research to 1955.

Woltereck, Richard. *Philosophie der lebendigen Wirklichkeit.* Vol. 1: *Grundzüge einer allgemeinen Biologie;* Vol. 2: *Ontologie des Lebendigen* (2nd ed., Stuttgart, 1940).

Wundt, M. *Kant als Metaphysiker* (Stuttgart, 1924).

Zimmer, Ernst. *Umsturz im Weltbild der Physik* (München, 1942).

INDEX